THE
MAN UTD
MISCELLANY

THE
MAN UTD
MISCELLANY

BY ANDY MITTEN

Vision Sports Publishing
2 Coombe Gardens,
London SW20 0QU

www.visionsp.co.uk

Published by Vision Sports Publishing. 2007

Text © Andy Mitten
Illustrations © Bob Bond Sporting Caricatures

ISBN 10: 1-905326-27-0
ISBN 13: 978-1905326-27-3

Printed and bound in the UK by
Cromwell Press Ltd, Trowbridge, Wiltshire

Typeset by Palimpsest Book Production Limited,
Grangemouth, Stirlingshire

A CIP catalogue record for this book is
available from the British Library

Mixed Sources
Product group from well-managed
forests and other controlled sources
www.fsc.org Cert no. TT-COC-2082
© 1996 Forest Stewardship Council

Vision Sports Publishing are
proud that this book is made
from paper certified by the
Forest Stewardship Council

Foreword
By Paddy Crerand

The passion of United fans for facts and figures never ceases to amaze me.

I'm lucky enough to watch the team home and away, to walk the streets outside stadiums and mingle with fans. Because I am a former player who contributed a small part to Manchester United's incredible history, fans recognise and approach me. They say all kinds of things. Some reminisce about games I played in and talk through events bit by bit with incredible clarity. Often they remember more than I did. Other fans ask me questions about other players. "What was George Best really like?" they'll say. While others try to catch me out by asking me United related trivia questions. They assume that because I played for the team then I must know more than them – which isn't always true.

It's no different at home. My two sons, who have watched United home and away for years, are always talking about the goings on at the club and my phone rings all the time – usually family and friends calling to talk about United. We'll go over transfer speculation and talk about the form of the team. We'll discuss the game we've just been to and the one we're about to go to. For nine months of the season it's an endless cycle of football, football and football. And while my wife may not agree with me, I wouldn't have it any other way.

I have learned a lot from reading this book, because I was never one for facts and figures as a player. I was always too busy preparing for my next game to pore over statistics about which player had provided the most crosses. And anyway, when I played in the late 1950's, 60's and early 70's, there wasn't the wealth of information that there is now, where if a player blinks then someone probably records it. I would look at the league table and that was about it. As long as United were winning, that was enough for me.

Fans often remember more than the players because they spend so much time reading up on the team and absorbing statistics. While I was mentally preparing for a game, fans were sat on the terraces reading the match day programme. But as I've got older I've come to appreciate important milestones and statistics. I find the little nuances fascinating, which is why it's so hard to put this little red book down once you've picked it up.

When I look at my own career, certain curiosities stand out. I signed for United on 6th February 1963, the fifth anniversary of the Munich air disaster, yet I didn't make my competitive debut for three weeks because the weather was so bad in England that all fixtures were postponed. I played over 400 games for United and scored just 15 goals. With players like Bobby, George Best, Denis Law and David Herd in front of me, tackling, playing through balls and defending were my priority rather than scoring.

I played alongside Bobby Charlton in midfield and Bobby was such a Manchester United institution, playing between 1956–73 and making 757 appearances, scoring 249 goals. I never thought anyone would surpass his appearance record for United, yet over three decades after he retired there's a real chance than Ryan Giggs will do that. For a player to stay at one club for so long in the modern game is truly staggering. I still think that Bobby's goalscoring record in safe, though.

Enjoy the book, and I hope you enjoy reading it as much as I did.

Paddy Crerand

Acknowledgements

I'd like to thank Iain McCartney, who is such a font of knowledge, facts and figures about United that we gave him his own 'Ask the Anorak' column in *United We Stand*. Iain, who runs the United Review Collectors' Club, was great source of help in compiling this book. I know Iain would like to thank his wife Linda and daughter Kelly for being so patient when he was working on this book, buried under a pile of newspaper cuttings, often late at night, in Anorak Towers.

I'd also like to thank Adam Renton, a longstanding Red, for putting the hours in before he put a backpack on and went to Asia to teach Mancunian English to kids in South-East Asia. Joyce Woolridge was assiduous as ever and Jim White's ideas were bang on as usual.

Jim Drewett and Toby Trotman at VSP were once again great to work with, while Clive Batty was a meticulous reader.

Andy Mitten

Author's Note: All the stats in *The Man Utd Miscellany* are correct up until the start of the 2007/08 season.

— IN THE BEGINNING —

The football club that became Manchester United was formed as Newton Heath L&YR FC in 1878. The club was the works team of the Lancashire and Yorkshire railway depot at Newton Heath.

The club's first ground, between 1878 and 1893, was at North Road, now Northampton Road, in Newton Heath, near the future site of Piccadilly Station. The team changed half a mile away at the Three Crowns public house and the pitch was located on the edge of a clay pit. Today, the North Manchester Business Park lies where the pitch once stood. Previously, Moston Brook High School stood on the site and a plaque pointed out the site's significance – until it was stolen.

By 1893 the club had entered the Football League and begun to sever its links with the railway company, dropping L &YR from its name. The Heathens, as they were known, also moved to a less cramped home three miles away in Clayton in September 1893. Located amongst billowing factories, the setting was pure Lowry-scape. Today, the old pitch is a car park for the Manchester Velodrome, marked by a red plaque on Bank Street. Manchester City's new stadium is but a Schmeichel kick away.

By the turn of the century, however, Newton Heath were in serious financial trouble with debts of more than £2,500. But at a meeting in the New Islington Hall, Ancoats, in 1901, Harry Stafford, the club's full-back, revealed a plan to save Newton Heath from bankruptcy. Legend has it that a local brewer called John Davies had stopped to admire Stafford's dog. Stafford had explained the club's plight and Davies had suggested clearing its debt and his becoming chairman.

The offer was accepted and at an early board meeting Davies suggested a new red and white strip and a new name to reflect the club's new start. Manchester Central and Manchester Celtic were considered, but eventually the name of Manchester United was decided upon, the new club coming into official existence on April 26th 1902.

— RED, WHITE AND BLACK —

Since switching from the green and gold of Newton Heath in 1902, the Manchester United strip has traditionally been red shirts, white shorts and black socks (see *United Home Kits 1878–2009*, centre page). However, there have been several notable occasions when this has not been the case.

- For the 1909 FA Cup final victory against Bristol City (whose traditional kit was also red shirts and white shorts), United ran out in white shirts with a red 'V' and white shorts. These colours were then adopted as first choice kit for three seasons between 1922 and 1926, before the club reverted to its traditional colours.

- On May 5th 1934, United had to beat Millwall in the last game of the season to avoid relegation to Division Three. Hoping for a change in the bad fortune that had dogged them all year, they decided to discard their famous red jerseys and instead wore cherry and white hoops. The plan worked, United won 2–0, and they never wore the strip again.

- When United beat Benfica to become the first team to lift the European Cup at Wembley in 1968, they were wearing an unfamiliar all blue strip (Benfica played in red and white).

— THE WISDOM OF SIR MATT —

"I believe you are seeking a team manager? Well, I am interested."
To the United chairman in 1945

"It was not an easy assignment. The ground had been blitzed, they had an overdraft at the bank, and what is more I had no experience as a manager and I felt they were taking a great risk in appointing me. All I had, apart from playing experience, was ideas about what a manager should do, faith in those ideas and faith for the future of the club."
On taking over at United

"I give you the answer in three words: skill, fitness and character; and the greatest of these is character."
On the key attributes of a United player

"Some people called me a visionary, others a reactionary, while a few called me awkward or stubborn."
After taking United into Europe, when the Football League was against such a move

"Prestige alone demanded that the continental challenge should be met, not avoided."
On Europe

"Every manager should have a hobby. Mine is soccer."

"Every manager should have a hobby. Mine is soccer!"

"So many good things in life have come my way since I became a professional footballer, it sometimes does me good to think back on the day when living was not so easy. It helps me keep my feet on the ground."

"I would hate to be the man who has to follow Matt Busby as manager at United."
City manager Joe Mercer

— DUNCAN IN THE DOCK —

Duncan Edwards was once fined 10 shillings (50p) by a court for riding his bicycle at night without any lights.

3

— UNITED NATIONS —

United have a long tradition of representation at the biggest football event on the planet. The following players were all Reds when they travelled to the World Cup as members of their respective national squads:

Year	Venue	Players
1950	Brazil	(3) John Aston, Henry Cockburn (England)
1954	Switzerland	(2) Roger Byrne, Tommy Taylor (England)
1958	Sweden	(3) Bobby Charlton (England), Harry Gregg (Northern Ireland), Colin Webster (Wales)
1962	Chile	(1) Bobby Charlton (England)
1966	England	(3) Bobby Charlton, John Connelly Nobby Stiles (England)
1970	Mexico	(3) Bobby Charlton, Alex Stepney, Nobby Stiles (England)
1974	West Germany	(3) Jim Holton, Martin Buchan, Willie Morgan (Scotland)
1978	Argentina	(4) Martin Buchan, Gordon McQueen, Joe Jordan, Lou Macari (Scotland)
1982	Spain	(4) Steve Coppell, Bryan Robson, Ray Wilkins (England), Norman Whiteside (Northern Ireland)
1986	Mexico	(7) Gary Bailey, Bryan Robson (England), Norman Whiteside (Northern Ireland), John Sivebaek, Jesper Olsen (Denmark), Gordon Strachan, Arthur Albiston (Scotland)
1990	Italy	(3) Bryan Robson, Neil Webb (England), Jim Leighton (Scotland).
1994	USA	(2) Dennis Irwin, Roy Keane (Ireland)
1998	France	(8) David Beckham, Teddy Sheringham, Gary Neville, Paul Scholes (England), Ronny Johnsen, Henning Berg, Ole Gunnar Solskjaer (Norway), Peter Schmeichel (Denmark)
2002	Japan/ South Korea	(10) David Beckham, Paul Scholes, Wes Brown, Nicky Butt (England), Mikael Silvestre, Fabien Barthez (France), Diego Forlan (Uruguay), Quinton Fortune (South Africa), Roy Keane* (Ireland), Juan Sebastian Veron (Argentina)

2006 Germany (12) Gary Neville, Rio Ferdinand, Wayne Rooney (England), Gabriel Heinze (Argentina), Cristiano Ronaldo (Portugal), Edwin Van der Sar, Ruud van Nistelrooy (Holland), Nemanja Vidic (Serbia and Montenegro), Tim Howard (USA), Mikael Silvestre, Louis Saha (France), Ji-Sung Park (South Korea)

*Left the squad prior to the tournament.

— RED HOT REDS —

United's biggest victories*:

Football League 10–1 v Wolves, October 15th 1892, North Road

Premiership 9–0 v Ipswich, March 4th 1995, Old Trafford

FA Cup 8–0 v Yeovil (fifth round), February 12th 1949, Maine Road

League Cup 7–2 v Newcastle (fourth round), October 27th 1976, Old Trafford

Charity Shield 8–4 v Swindon September 25th 1911, Stamford Bridge

European Cup 10–0 v Anderlecht (Preliminary round, second leg), September 26th 1956, Maine Road

Champions League 7–1 v Roma, Champions League (quarter final), April 10th 2007

UEFA/Fairs Cup 6–1 v Djurgardens (first round, second leg), October 27th 1964, Old Trafford
6–1 v Borussia Dortmund (second round, first leg), November 11th 1964, Rote Erde Stadion

Cup Winners' Cup 6–1 v Willem II (first round, second leg), October 15th 1963, Old Trafford

* By margin of scoreline.

United's three highest aggregate scores in European competition:

1956/57 European Cup v Anderlecht, 12–0 (H 10–0 A 2–0)

1964/65 Inter Cities Fairs Cup v Borussia Dortmund, 10–1 (H 4–0 A 6–1)

1998/99 Champions League v Brondby, 11–2 (H 5–0 A 6–2)

— MADE FOR MANAGEMENT —

Maybe there is something about life at United that prepares players for management after leaving Old Trafford. Here are some ex-Reds who make their living picking other teams:

Gordon Strachan (Glasgow Celtic)
Steve Coppell (Reading)
Mark Hughes (Blackburn Rovers)
Steve Bruce (Birmingham City)
Roy Keane (Sunderland)
Paul Ince (MK Dons)
Darren Ferguson (Peterborough United)
Chris Casper (Bury)
Sammy McIlroy (Morecambe)
Brian Carey (Wrexham)

— KEEPING IT IN THE FAMILY —

When Phil Neville made his first-team debut in a 5–2 FA Cup fourth round victory over Wrexham at Old Trafford in January 1995, he was following in the footsteps of older brother Gary, who first pulled on a red shirt three years earlier against Torpedo Moscow in the UEFA Cup.

The pair started a United game together for the first time on August 19th 1995 in a 3–1 defeat to Aston Villa at Villa Park, making them the first set of brothers to simultaneously represent United since Jimmy and Brian Greenhoff in the 1970s.

The Greenhoffs first played together for United in a 1–1 draw with Leicester at Filbert Street on November 20th 1976 and were both in the starting line-up as United captured the FA Cup later that season, Jimmy scoring in the final against Liverpool. The Nevilles matched this feat, when they started United's 2–0 win over Newcastle in the 1999 FA Cup final (Phil was given the nod ahead of Gary in the 1996 win over Liverpool).

The Nevilles are a renowned sporting family: father Neville Neville (yes, that really is his name!) was once commercial director of Bury FC, while sister Tracey represented England at netball.

The Nevilles and Greenhoffs are two of six sets of brothers to play for United at the same time. Roger and Jack Doughty were the first to do so between 1890 and 1891, followed by Fred and Harry Erentz (1898), James and John Hodge (1913) and Martin and George Buchan (1973).

Sir Bobby Charlton may never have played with brother Jack at club level but the siblings were World Cup winners with England in 1966 – a feat matched only by Fritz and Ottmar Walter who won the Jules Rimet trophy with Germany in 1954.

John Aston senior and his son, John Aston junior both came through United's youth ranks to play for the first team, with considerable success. Aston senior won the FA Cup in 1948, while Aston junior won the title in 1967 and the European Cup a year later.

— NICKNAMES XI —

Dracula (Paddy Roche)
Busby a.k.a. Nosy (Paul Parker)
Larry White (Laurent Blanc)
The Black Pearl of Inchicore (Paul McGrath)
Sunbed (Clayton Blackmore)
Boom Boom (Duncan Edwards)
Stroller (George Graham)
Knocker (Enoch West)
Merlin (Gordon Hill)
The Judge (Lou Macari)
Choccy (Brian McClair)

Manager: **Mr Bojangles** (Ron Atkinson)

— RED GOOGLIES —

Number of web site pages produced by a Google search for the following United-related names:

Cristiano Ronaldo	3,010,000
Wayne Rooney	1,830,000
Eric Cantona	586,000
Malcolm Glazer	231,000
Duncan Edwards	112,000
Denis Law	93,500
Jim Leighton	23,500
William Prunier	888
Pete Boyle	734
Giuliano Maiorana	76

— DOUBLE TROUBLE —

Only four clubs have managed to beat United home and away in the same season since the formation of the Premier League. Here are those that have managed it:

	Old Trafford	Away
1993/94 Chelsea	0–1	0–1
1997/98 Arsenal	0–1	2–3
2000/01 Liverpool	0–1	0–2
2001/02 Arsenal	0–1	1–3
2001/02 Liverpool	0–1	1–3
2004/05 Chelsea	0–1	1–3
2005/06 Blackburn Rovers	1–2	3–4
2006/07 Arsenal	0–1	1–2

— RED NOTES —

Musicians and pop stars who follow United:

Mick Hucknall
David Gray
Mani (Stone Roses, Primal Scream)
Ian Brown
Terry Hall (The Specials)
Russell Watson
Bez (Happy Mondays)
Ed O'Brien (Radiohead)
Mark Collins (Charlatans)
Richard Ashcroft (The Verve)
Simon Webb (Blue)
Cerys Matthews (Catatonia)
Kym Marsh (Hearsay)

— SPORTING REDS —

United fans who have achieved success in other sports:

Geoffrey Boycott (cricket)
Michael Atherton (cricket)
Darren Campbell (athletics)
Ken Doherty, John Virgo (snooker)

— KEANO! —

Keano, Keano!

Some memorable Roy Keane moments:

- His finest hour. Juventus, Turin 1999. Two-nil down against the team perceived to be the best in Europe, a Keano-inspired United fight back to win 3–2. Roy is booked for his troubles and misses the final. His Herculean effort is still regarded by many Reds as the greatest individual performance they've ever seen. Roy reckons he did "alright."
- Maine Road, 1993. Galatasaray have knocked United out of Europe three days before and City fans shower the United players with bars of Turkish delight in the warm up. City are 2–0 up at

half time. Cantona scores. Twice. Then Irwin puts a far post cross behind the City defenders and Keane, having timed his run perfectly, puts the ball away with a half-volley. 3–2.

- The City Ground, 1991. A minute into the start of the game, the then Nottingham Forest midfielder goes for a 50/50 ball with Bryan Robson. He clatters Robson and wins the ball. Sir Alex later said: "I couldn't believe the cheek of it." But Keane had marked Ferguson's card.

- Middlesbrough at Old Trafford, 2000. With the score 0–0, United need a win. Referee Andy D'Urso awards a penalty to 'Boro. Keane disputes the decision and charges towards the referee, the veins in his neck bulging. D'Urso keeps retreating; Keane keeps advancing, keeps pleading, an image wired around the world. He later said: "The photographs were shocking. The psycho in them was me. I know we were wrong, I the worst offender."

- Hale 2002. The media are camping outside Keane's house after his World Cup walkout. His wife says, "The dog hasn't been out for a couple of days." So he walks the dog, chased by a pack of unfit journalists whom he ignores. "I thought Triggs was going to bite some of them," said Roy later.

- Mayfield, Cork 1997. Roy marries Theresa in Mayfield, Cork. Just 15 immediate family members attend. No photos of the wedding appear in *OK!* or *Hello!*.

- Highbury, 2005. Roy accuses 6ft 4ins Patrick Vieira of trying to intimidate 5ft 11ins Gary Neville in the tunnel before the game. Roy intervenes and tells Vieira in his lilting Cork patois to pick on someone his own size. Like him. Roy is the same height as Gary Neville. Roy goes on to be man of the match, described by Sir Alex as the best the Premiership has ever seen.

- Following defeat in Munich in 2001, Keane tells a journalist that the present team, "are not good enough. Maybe we need to break it up, get new players, start again." The first of the 'Keane Slams Team-mates' headlines is born. What they didn't point out was that he was including himself as being in that comfort zone.

- Following a draw with Dinamo Kiev in 2000, played in front of a dire Old Trafford atmosphere, Keane says, "Our fans away from home are as good as any, but at home you sometimes wonder if they understand the game of football. Some people come to Old Trafford and I don't think they can even spell the word football, let alone understand it. Away from home our fans are fantastic, what I would call the hardcore fans, but at home they've had a few drinks and probably their prawn sandwiches and don't realize what is going on out on the pitch. It's right out of order."

- 1993. Roy agrees to join Blackburn Rovers for £4m. He calls Ewood Park on Friday afternoon, but the offices are closed and he is told to wait until Monday to sign the contract. That weekend Alex Ferguson makes contact. The rest is history. Blackburn manager Kenny Dalglish is furious and threatens to sue Keane for every penny he has. He doesn't.
- November 2005 and Roy goes on MUTV to give a standard player interview. Except no such thing exists as far as the outspoken Keane is concerned. The United captain is so critical of some of his team-mates that the transmission is pulled by United's top suits. A week later, Keane leaves Old Trafford after over 12 years at the club.

— SERIE A XI —

A team of United players who have also played in Italy:

1 Edwin Van der Sar (Juventus)
2 Jaap Stam (Lazio, Milan)
3 Laurent Blanc (Inter)
4 Mikael Silvestre (Inter)
5 Lee Sharpe (Sampdoria)
6 Andrei Kanchelskis (Fiorentina)
7 Ray Wilkins (Milan)
8 Juan Sebastian Veron (Sampdoria, Parma, Lazio, Inter)
9 Joe Jordan (Milan)
10 Denis Law (Torino)
11 Carlo Sartori (Bologna, Spal, Lecce, Rimini)

— UNITED ON FILM —

- Modern footballers may be as famous as Hollywood movie stars but United winger Billy Meredith set a precedent for Reds appearing on the big screen as long ago as 1926, when he starred in a little-known British silent film called *Ball of Fortune*. Only 30 seconds of footage survives at the National Film Archive, in which we see Meredith's famed wing wizardry.
- Children's Film Foundation classic *Cup Fever* (1965) tells the story of Barton United, a junior side whose attempts to win the cup are held back by the father of a rival player's team. Things do not look good until Matt Busby, George Best, Bobby Charlton, Denis Law and Nobby Stiles turn up to help them out.

- Old Trafford features in the Albert Finney film, *Charlie Bubbles* (1967) when a child watches a game from an executive box at the ground.
- A sadistic PE teacher played by Brian Glover acts out his fantasy of being Bobby Charlton on a school playing field in Ken Loach's adaptation of the novel *Kes* (1969).
- United supporters were used as unwitting extras during an FA Cup tie against Sheffield United at Bramall Lane, when filming took place at half-time for *When Saturday Comes* (1996), a predictable zero-to-hero football tale starring Blades fan Sean Bean.
- Bean's performance was not nearly as wooden as some of those in *Beyond the Promised Land* (2000), a supposed fly-on-the-wall documentary officially sanctioned by United that follows the team during 1999/00. 'Highlights' include Roy Keane getting angry when he suspects Sir Alex Ferguson of fixing a quiz and 'negotiations' between the club and Vodafone over sponsorship.
- David Beckham's iconic free-kicks ensured that there was only one player's name suitable for director Gurinder Chadha's 2002 film, *Bend It Like Beckham*, the story of a Sikh girl determined to play football. Beckham did not appear alongside stars Parminder Nagra and Keira Knightley, although he has popped up on the silver screen – as a Real Madrid player – in the *Goal!* trilogy.
- The subject of a plethora of biographies and autobiographies, George Best's life story was told in Mary McGuikian's biopic, *Best* (2000). This dire effort is no reflection on the real Best, who is captured beautifully in *Fussball Wie Noch Nie* (Football As Never Before) – a documentary of his individual performance against Coventry City on September 12th, 1970. Best was also the inspiration for *Dari Jemapoh Ke Manchestee* (From Jemapoh to Manchester) (1998), a Malaysian road movie about United fans besotted with his image. Sick Boy also refers to Best in the adaptation of Irvine Welsh's novel *Trainspotting* (1996): "At one time you've got it and then you lose it and it's gone forever. All walks of life: George Best, for example. Had it, lost it."
- In the 1972 film *The Lovers*, a spin-off from the TV sitcom of the same name, Richard Beckinsale (later Lennie Godber in *Porridge*) played Geoffrey, a Manchester bank clerk with twin obsessions – Manchester United and losing his virginity with girlfriend Beryl, played by Paula Wilcox. He tried unsuccessfully to unite his two objects of desire by inviting Beryl on a date which turns out to be on the terraces at Old Trafford.

— BRICK BY BRICK —

Key years in the development of Old Trafford:

1910: Old Trafford opens. It holds 80,000 and has cover on one side, the main stand.

1934: A roof is built over the United Road terrace opposite. It is later damaged during the war.

1959: The Stretford End terrace is covered. It becomes a focal point for vocal Reds.

1965: The cantilever stand on the United Road side opens in time for the World Cup.

1972: 'K' Stand opens behind the goal, almost linking the United Road with the main stand. Security fencing is added around the pitch two years later.

1985: The family stand opens. Three-quarters of Old Trafford is now unified by a sleek cantilevered stand. Along with Goodison Park, it is the only ground in Britain with standing and seating on all four sides. Capacity is 58,000.

1986: The club museum opens and the giant floodlights are dismantled the following season.

1992: The Stretford End terrace is demolished and replaced by an all-seater stand. Ground capacity is 44,800.

1995: Britain's biggest stand, the 25,300 seat triple tiered North Stand is built. Capacity rises to 55,500.

2000: New tiers holding 6,000 each are added behind both goals. Capacity is now 67,800.

2006: The corners between the new tiers and the north stand are filled in adding an extra 7,500 seats. Old Trafford now holds 76,400, just 3,600 short of the Bernabeu in Madrid. Plans are already underfoot to add two new quadrants, raising the capacity to around 85,000.

— MATCH ABANDONED —

The last United fixture to be abandoned was the league game against Manchester City at Old Trafford on April 27th 1974. Denis Law's late backheeled goal for City caused a mass pitch invasion as fans expressed their dismay at United's relegation from the top flight. The Football League awarded City three points.

The last United game which was abandoned and needed a replay was in December 1962 when a match at Old Trafford against Arsenal was halted after 57 minutes due to fog. United were leading 1–0 at the time, but lost the rearranged fixture 3–2.

— EUROPEAN DEFEATS —

United's proud unbeaten home record in European competition was finally ended by Fenerbahce on October 30th 1996, when a goal from Fredi Bobic gave the Turkish champions a 1–0 win at Old Trafford in the Champions League group stage. The record had stood for 40 years and 57 games. With the expansion of the Champions League and therefore more European games, United have suffered six further home reverses since then. They are:

0–1 v Juventus (Champions League Group Stage, November 20th 1996)

0–1 v Borussia Dortmund (Champions League semi-final 2nd leg, April 23rd 1997)

2–3 v Real Madrid (Champions League quarter-final 2nd leg, April 19th 2000)

0–1 v Bayern Munich (Champions League quarter-final 1st leg, April 3rd 2001)

2–3 v Deportivo La Coruña (Champions League Group Stage, October 17th 2001)

0–1 v Milan (Champions League 2nd rd 1st leg, February 23rd 2005)

— PAPER TALK —

Slow news day? Then expect the British press to tell us that such-and-such a player is definitely about to join United. The following XI (named along with their employers at the time) would all have worn red under Sir Alex Ferguson if those 'exclusive' red-top stories were to be believed:

1 Gianluigi Buffon (Juventus)
2 Lillian Thuram (Parma)
3 Tony Adams (Arsenal)
4 Miguel Angel Nadal (Barcelona)
5 Roberto Carlos (Real Madrid)
6 Manuel Rui Costa (Fiorentina)
7 Paul Gascoigne (Newcastle)
8 Gennaro Gattusso (Milan)
9 Arjen Robben (PSV)
10 Gabriel Batistuta (Fiorentina)
11 Ronaldo (Inter)

Coach: Marcello Lippi (Juventus)

— MEDIA REDS —

A selection of ex-Reds who have forged a career in the media:

Garth Crooks (BBC)
Eamon Dunphy (RTE and ghost writer of Roy Keane's autobiography)
Paddy Crerand (MUTV)
Gordon McQueen (Sky)
Lou Macari (MUTV and Century FM)
George Graham (Sky)
Frank Stapleton (Sky)
Ray Wilkins (Sky)
Ron Atkinson (ex-ITV)
Mickey Thomas (MUTV, Century FM)
Denis Irwin (MUTV)
Arthur Albiston (BBC Radio Manchester)

— BATTLE OF BRITAIN —

United have played against British opposition in Europe just six times, never losing a one-off match or a tie over two legs. Here is United's complete record against British clubs in European competition:

Season	Opponent	Competition	Home	Away
1963/64	Tottenham Hotspur	Cup Winners' Cup	4–1	0–2
1964/65	Everton	Fairs Cup	1–1	2–1
1984/85	Dundee United	UEFA Cup	2–2	3–2
1990/91	Wrexham	Cup Winners' Cup	3–0	2–0
2003/04	Rangers	Champions League	3–0	1–0
2006/07	Celtic	Champions League	3–2	0–1

— ALTERNATIVE CAREERS —

A Google search on these United players reveals what their namesakes do for a living:

Wayne M. Rooney, private detective in Florida
Wes Brown, actor
Darren Fletcher, retired Major League baseball player
John O'Shea, musician from Australia
Michael Carrick, computing officer at Newcastle University

— FA CUP WINNING CAPTAINS —

Bryan Robson has lifted the FA Cup on three occasions

Only eight players have lifted the FA Cup as United captain, with Bryan Robson achieving the feat on a hat-trick of occasions. Here's the full list:

Charlie Roberts	1909
Johnny Carey	1948
Noel Cantwell	1963
Martin Buchan	1977
Bryan Robson	1983, 1985, 1990
Steve Bruce	1994
Eric Cantona	1996
Roy Keane	1999, 2004

— OLD TRAFFORD FINALS —

United's home ground has hosted several showpiece finals not involving United, including:

Date	Final	Result	Attendance
April 26th 1911	FA Cup (replay)	Bradford City 1–0 Newcastle	58,000
April 24th 1915	FA Cup	Sheffield United 3–0 Chelsea	49,557
April 11th 1970	FA Cup (replay)	Chelsea 2–1 Leeds (aet)	62,708
April 13th 1977	League Cup (2nd replay)	Aston Villa 3–2 Everton (aet)	54,749
March 22nd 1978	League Cup (replay)	Nottingham Forest 1–0 Liverpool	54,375
May 28th 2003	Champions League Final	Milan 0–0 Juventus (aet, Milan won 3–2 on penalties)	62,315

In addition, rugby league's Super League grand finals have been held at Old Trafford in consecutive years since 1998.

— COUNT THE CROWD —

United may well have been English football's best supported team for 34 out of 56 post-war seasons but on the odd occasion Old Trafford has held some less than spectacularly sized crowds. Here are five home games where the Red Army failed to turn out in force:

Date	League	Result	Attendance
May 10th 1989	Division One	United 1 Everton 2	26,722
October 24th 1960	Division One	United 2 Nottm Forest 1	23,628
May 2nd 1989	Division One	United 1 Wimbledon 0	23,368
February 23rd 1955	Division One	United 2 Wolves 4	15,679
February 5th 1947	Division One	United 1 Stoke City 1	8,456*

*Played at Maine Road

— CLUB WORLD CHAMPIONSHIP —

After winning the European Cup for the first time in 1968, United played South American champions Estudiantes for the Intercontinental Club Cup. The ill-tempered tie was played over two legs with the Argentinian side winning 1–0 at La Bombanera in Buenos Aires, before holding United to a 1–1 draw at Old Trafford.

Having won the Champions League 31 years later in 1999, United controversially decided to pull out of the FA Cup in January 2000 to take part in FIFA's inaugural Club World Championship in Brazil, determined to prove that they were the greatest club side on the planet. However, after winning the Intercontinental Club Cup with a Roy Keane-inspired 1–0 victory over Palmeiras in Tokyo two months previously, Sir Alex Ferguson's side wilted in the South American heat, failing to qualify from the group stages.

United played just three games in the Maracana stadium in Rio. Dwight Yorke scored in a 1–1 draw with Mexican side Rayos del Necaxa, but the game will be better remembered for the sending off of David Beckham, who was shown a red card for violent conduct.

Brazilians Vasco Da Gama then outclassed the Reds, winning 3–1 in front of a crowd of 73,000. Nicky Butt scored for United but a goal from Edmundo and two from Romario after elementary errors by Gary Neville saw the Reds dumped out of the competition. "Obrigado [Thanks] Neville!" exclaimed one Brazilian newspaper headline the next morning.

With their fate sealed, a weakened United team defeated South Melbourne 2–0 thanks to goals from Quinton Fortune. Meanwhile, Vasco made it to the final but were beaten by compatriots Corinthians 4–3 on penalties after the Paulistas had held United's conquerors to a 0–0 draw.

— JOHANNES HYACINTHUS RULES OK —

Sir Alexander **Chapman** Ferguson
David **Robert Joseph** Beckham
Eric **Daniel Pierre** Cantona
Arnold **Johannes Hyacinthus** Muhren
Peter **Boleslaw** Schmeichel
Paul **Emerson Carlyle** Ince
Roy **Maurice** Keane
Sammy **Baxter** McIlroy
Mickey **Reginald** Thomas

— STRETFORD END BANNERS —

'31 YEARS':
Reference to the length of time that rivals Manchester City have gone
without a trophy (their last piece of silverware was the League Cup
in 1976). The banner is updated on an annual basis with stick-on
Velcro digits.

'FEBRUARY 6 1958 – THE FLOWERS OF MANCHESTER'
The title of a song by The Spinners, this is a tribute to the eight United
players that died in the Munich Air Disaster (see *The Flowers of
Manchester*, page 36).

'ONE LOVE – STRETFORD END – MUFC'
Another musical reference, 'One Love', is a song by Manchester band
the Stone Roses.

'MUFC THE RELIGION'
Loyal, devoted, fanatical. That's United's support.

'REPUBLIC OF MANCUINIA – RED ARMY'
Written in Cyrillic font, this banner sums up the separatist sentiments
of some United fans.

'20 LEGEND'
A tribute to Ole Gunnar Solskjaer, cleverly making use of the
Norwegian striker's squad number.

— THE LONG WAIT —

Some United supporters thought the team would never end its quest
for the league title as they endured 26 years without being crowned
Kings of England between 1967 and 1993. But that is not the longest
period that Reds have had to wait to see their team win the league.

Despite forming in 1878, Newton Heath were not admitted to the
Football League until 1892/93 and spent their first three years of league
football in the Football Alliance. They never won a title, but after
becoming Manchester United in 1902, finally captured the league in
1908 – 30 years after their formation.

United were champions again in 1911 but endured a 41-year
absence from the top spot in a period punctuated by two World Wars,
before becoming champions again in 1952. Thankfully, the club has
not suffered for such a long time ever since.

— THE FOOTBALL LEAGUE CUP —

The Football League Cup – in its various names and guises – has often been overlooked by United, with the three-handled trophy deemed the least important of any that the Reds challenge for each year.

Although they took part in the inaugural tournament in 1960/61, losing to Bradford City in the second round, United then declined to take part for a further five consecutive seasons. After re-joining the competition in 1966/67 the Reds' stay was short-lived, as they were knocked out by Blackpool, suffering a 5–1 defeat at Bloomfield Road.

Again, United chose not to enter the following season and did not re-enter until 1969/70, when the promise of a UEFA Cup place for the winners was too good a chance to turn down.

The League Cup remained something of an unloved after-thought, with United not reaching the final until 1983. Under Sir Alex Ferguson the Reds have won the cup twice and reached the final on a further two occasions, although the Scot has often used the competition as an opportunity to give young players their United debuts and to rest more experienced regulars.

United's League Cup final appearances:

Date	Result	Venue	Attendance
March 26th 1983	United 1 Liverpool 2	Wembley	100,000
April 21st 1991	United 0 Sheffield Wednesday 1	Wembley	77,612
April 12th 1992	United 1 Nottingham Forest 0	Wembley	76,810
March 27th 1994	United 1 Aston Villa 3	Wembley	77,231
March 2nd 2003	United 0 Liverpool 2	Millennium Stadium	74,500
February 26th 2006	United 4 Wigan 0	Millennium Stadium	66,866

— RUUD'S EURO RECORD —

Ruud van Nistelrooy's 12 goals in the 2002/03 Champions League competition remain a tournament record. His goals came against Bayer Leverkusen (3), Maccabi Haifa (1), Basle (2), Deportivo (2), Juventus (2) and Real Madrid (2). For good measure, van Nistelrooy also scored twice against Hungarian tongue-twisters Zalaegerszeg in the qualifying round.

— TRYING TO REPLACE THE IRREPLACEABLE —

Goalkeepers who have made first-team appearances for United since Peter Schmeichel's retirement in 1999:

Raimond Van der Gouw
Nick Culkin
Paul Rachubka
Mark Bosnich
Massimo Taibi
Andy Goram
Fabien Barthez
Ricardo
Tim Howard
Roy Carroll
Edwin van der Sar
Tomasz Kuszczak
John O'Shea (stand-in)

— UNITED LADIES (RIP) —

Manchester United Ladies were formed in 1977 but never enjoyed anything like the success of their male counterparts during a 28-year history. The female Reds only became an official part of the club at the start of 2001/02, playing in the third tier of English women's football, the Northern Combination League. The side was disbanded at the end of 2004/05, with United preferring to channel funds into their football in the community scheme, rather than a competitive women's team.

— WORLD CUP WINNERS —

United players who have won the World Cup:

England 1966: Sir Bobby Charlton (1954–73), Nobby Stiles (1960–71) and John Connelly* (1964–66)
France 1998: Fabien Barthez (2000–03) and Laurent Blanc* (2001–03)
Brazil 2002: Kleberson (2002–05)

* Didn't play in final

— GEORGE BEST: A LIFE REMEMBERED —

"He had the lot"

"The closest I got to him was when we shook hands at the end of the game."
Roy Fairfax, Best's marker when he scored six goals in the 8–2 FA Cup win against Northampton Town in February 1970

"George was the most naturally gifted player I have ever seen. He had the lot; balance, pace, two good feet, he was brave strong, strong and a good header of the ball. Pele wasn't as gifted as George Best. He couldn't beat players in as many ways as George could."
Johnny Giles, United team-mate

"Anyone who witnessed what George could do wished they could do the same. He was on a par, at least, with anyone. From a talent and

style point of view, I would say that Cruyff was probably the nearest thing to him. But George was braver."
Sir Bobby Charlton

"We had our problems with the wee fella, but I prefer to remember the genius."
Sir Matt Busby

"With feet as sensitive as a pickpocket's hands, his control of the ball under the most violent pressure was hypnotic. The bewildering repertoire of feints and swerves . . . and balance that would have made Isaac Newton decide he might as well have eaten the apple."
Hugh McIlvanney, journalist

"People used to say he was just into booze and women, but . . . he was one of the best trainers I've ever seen. He had to be to be able to do the things he did."
Derek Doogan, Northern Ireland team-mate

"What George did was to show that tactics and formations are for the majority of us, while the genius plays the game in a way that is simply beyond the mere mortals."
Graham Taylor

"It seems impossible to hurt him. All manner of men have tried to intimidate him. Best merely glides along, riding tackles and brushing giants aside like leaves."
Joe Mercer, former City manager

"George inspired me when I was young. He was flamboyant and exciting. I think we were very similar players – dribblers who could create moments of magic."
Diego Maradona

"George Best was the best player in the world, not just England, and a good friend of mine. I remember one day he played Benfica in 1966 in Lisbon. We lost 5–1 and George was spectacular, a genius."
Eusebio, former Benfica and Portugal star

"He has ice in his veins, warmth in his heart and timing and balance in his feet."
Danny Blanchflower, former Tottenham and Northern Ireland captain

— BEST ON BEST —

"If you could have given me the choice of beating four defenders and smashing a goal in from 30 yards or going to bed with Miss World, it would have been difficult. Luckily, I had both. It's just that you do one of those things in front of 50,000 people."

"People prefer loveable rogues to Mr Nice Guys. The real heroes are the mavericks, the people who play sport with a glint in their eye."

"That thing about being the fifth Beatle, I just found it so freaky. I was just a kid from the Cregagh Estate in Belfast trying to make sense of my life as a footballer and a person."

"I'd give all the champagne I've ever drunk to play alongside Eric Cantona in a big European match at Old Trafford."

"I was born with a great gift, and sometimes that comes with a destructive streak. Just as I wanted to outdo everyone when I played, I had to outdo everyone when we were out on the town."

— UNITED ON FILM, TAKE TWO! —

More films with a United connection . . .

- *Doppelganger* (2001) is a quirky animation in which Ryan Giggs is kidnapped by an evil genius and forced to play for Manchester City.
- *United* (2003) is a Norwegian film about Kare and Anna, two fanatical Reds who live in a small town on the west coast of Norway.
- Meteorologists watch a United match on television as global warming threatens to destroy the world in crazy weather blockbuster *The Day After Tomorrow* (2004).
- Cate Blanchett sports a United shirt and discusses the merits of Eric Cantona with Colin Farrell in the story of Irish journalist *Victoria Guerin* (2003).
- Cantona appeared in several films after he finished playing, including the Oscar-winning *Elizabeth* (1998), which also starred United fan Christopher Eccleston.
- Eccleston played DCI David Bilborough in television series *Cracker*, a policeman who supports United. Bilborough is murdered by Liverpool fan Albie, played by Robert Carlyle, in scenes filmed in and around Old Trafford.
- Former United player Harry McShane's son Ian McShane, perhaps best known as the television character Lovejoy, stars as a journeyman alcoholic footballer in *Yesterday's Hero* (1979).

— 'ISN'T THAT . . . ?' —

Yes, it is him: celebrity fans who have actually been seen at matches:

Christopher Eccleston: *Doctor Who* himself sets the Tardis down in the North Stand most home games.

Ian Brown: Art imitates life. Brown imitates his idol, George Best. Now has a season ticket in the East Lower with his kids.

Angus Deayton: Coke-snorting hooker user – and no allegedly about it.

Richard Wilson: He doesn't believe it when United lose.

Eamonn Holmes: Up with the lark every day, talking blarney.

Terry Christian: Former *The Word* presenter, professional Mancunian and Red author.

Tony Wilson: Factory Records and Hacienda nightclub founder, undisputed heavyweight champion of professional Mancunians, and a keen fanzine reader.

Bez: The Happy Mondays freaky dancer and, er, *Celebrity Big Brother* winner.

Debbie Horsfield: Top-notch television writer, responsible for *Cutting It*.

John Squire: Once of Manchester's finest, the Stone Roses.

Mani: Squire's old colleague and *Soccer AM* regular, now playing bass in Primal Scream.

Terry Hall: The former Specials man has kept the Red faith for three decades.

Mike Peters: Alarm frontman and dedicated north Wales Red.

— ON CLOUD NINE —

Here's how Andy Cole (5), Mark Hughes (2), Roy Keane and Paul Ince put United into the record books by scoring in the 9–0 victory over Ipswich on March 4th 1995 – the biggest in Premiership history:

1	16 mins: Keane	Right foot shot from edge of the area.
2	24 mins: Cole	Side foot from a Ryan Giggs cross.
3	37 mins: Cole	Tap-in after Hughes hit the bar.
4	53 mins: Cole	Strike from close range.
5	54 mins: Hughes	Powerful shot from another Giggs cross.
6	59 mins: Hughes	Close-range header.
7	65 mins: Cole	Nets rebound after a header from Brian McClair is saved.
8	73 mins: Ince	Chips keeper Craig Forrest with quickly taken free-kick.
9	89 mins: Cole	Shoots on the turn to claim his fifth.

— HAVEN'T WE SEEN YOU BEFORE? —

These Reds have all played both for and against United in the Champions League:

Eric Djemba-Djemba (Nantes)
Jesper Blomqvist (Gothenburg)
Mikael Silvestre (Inter)
Fabien Barthez (Monaco)
Henning Berg (Rangers)
Jordi Cruyff (Barcelona)
Karel Poborsky (Sparta Prague)

— WORST RUN OF LEAGUE FORM —

The Reds have twice gone 16 league games without a win – between November 3rd 1928 and February 13th 1929, and between April 19th and October 25th 1930. In the second of these dismal spells 14 of the games were defeats.

— JINGLE ALL AWAY —

United travelled to away grounds for the once traditional Christmas Day fixture on 10 occasions:

Year	League	Result	Attendance
1897	Division Two	1–0 v Manchester City*	16,000
1908	Division One	1–2 v Newcastle	35,000
1912	Division One	4–1 v Chelsea	33,000
1920	Division One	4–3 v Aston Villa	38,000
1924	Division Two	1–1 v Middlesbrough	18,500
1926	Division One	1–1 v Tottenham	37,287
1930	Division One	1–3 v Bolton	22,662
1946	Division One	2–2 v Bolton	28,505
1950	Division One	1–2 v Sunderland	41,215
1952	Division One	0–0 v Blackpool	27,778

*As Newton Heath

— NUMBERS GAME —

Clayton Blackmore wore every shirt number from 2–12 during his time at United.

— COMMERCIAL GAINS —

Some Manchester United Megastore facts:

- The Manchester United Megastore at Old Trafford occupies 13,562 feet.
- It employs 26 staff during the week with an extra 60 casual staff and 12 security personnel on match days.
- Around 30,000 fans visit on a matchday: nearly 40 per cent of the average attendance.
- 850,000 people visited during 2002/03.
- Around 1,500 different products are sold.

— SOME YEARS ARE LONGER THAN OTHERS —

In 1964/65 United played from the opening day season on August 22nd 1964 until a Fairs Cup semi-final replay with Ferencvaros on June 16th 1965 – their longest season ever. This total of nine months and 26 days is nine days longer than both 1967/68 and 1998/99, seasons when United were involved in European Cup finals.

— NOTABLE DEBUTS —

Bobby Charlton: Scored twice at Old Trafford on October 6th 1956 v Charlton Athletic.

Wayne Rooney: Scored a hat-trick on his United and Champions League debut on September 28th 2004 v Fenerbahce.

Harold Halse: Scored in first minute v Everton on April 8th 1908.

Steve Bruce: Gave away a penalty, was booked and broke his nose on December 19th 1987, away at Portsmouth.

Albert Pape: Travelled to Old Trafford with Clapton Orient on February 7th 1925, but was transferred to United an hour before kick-off.

Ole Gunnar Solskjaer: Scored six minutes after coming on as a substitute against Blackburn Rovers at Old Trafford on August 25th 1996.

Peter Beardsley: Substituted at half-time against Bournemouth in the League Cup on October 6th 1982 in his one and only United appearance. Went on to star for Newcastle, Liverpool, Everton and England.

Pat McGibbon: Sent off after 51 minutes of a 3–0 League Cup defeat to York City at Old Trafford on September 20th 1995. He never played for the first team again.

— WHEN THE SEAGULLS FOLLOW
THE TRAWLER . . . —

He didn't say much, but when he did . . .

Eric's words of wisdom:

"When the seagulls follow the trawler, it is because they think sardines will be thrown into the sea."

"It happens to us all that we get a little sad sometimes, we feel a little melancholy. But being melancholic can be a pleasure too. The human body above all needs to feel alive, and sometimes people can't feel the joy of great pleasure. So they take pleasure in sadness."

"I feel close to the rebelliousness and vigour of youth here . . . behind Manchester's windows, there is an insane love of football, celebration and music."

THE MAN UTD MISCELLANY

"The more the media try to manipulate opinion against me, the more people like me. When journalists attack me, they show their true colours. They reveal their hand and people are shocked. I'm a living witness to the fact that people are beginning to understand how power works."

"There's a fine line between freedom and chaos. To some extent I espouse the idea of anarchy. What I am really after is an anarchy of thought, a liberation of the mind from all convention."

"If there is something that frightens me, it's the idea that one day I'll die, that some day I'll simply disappear. And what frightens me isn't dying so much as not living any more. It's not the darkness of death that worries me, but the thought of no longer living existing in the bright light of living."

— GOOD GOAL BUT GOODBYE —

Three players have scored for United in their one and only game for the club: R. Stephenson in 1896, Bill Bainbridge in 1945 and Albert Kinsey in 1965.

— OLDEST EVER PLAYER —

Billy Meredith was 46 years and 281 days old when he played for United against Derby in 1921. Raimond van Der Gouw became United's oldest post-war player when he came on as a substitute for Andy Goram against Charlton Athletic on May 11th 2001, aged 39 years and 48 days.

— UNITED SUPPORTING CAST —

Actors who support the Reds include:

Andrew Lincoln: Egg in *This Life*
Christopher Eccleston: Former *Doctor Who* and acted alongside
Eric Cantona in *Elizabeth*
James Nesbitt: Adam in *Cold Feet*
Ralf Little: Antony in *The Royle Family*
Mark Charnock: *Emmerdale's* Marlon Dingle
Ian McShane: Title role in *Lovejoy*
Steve McFadden: Phil Mitchell in *EastEnders*
Robert Powell: Salfordian who played *Jesus of Nazareth*
John Simm: DI Sam Tyler in *Life on Mars*

— MANCHESTER UNITED OPUS —

In December 2006, Kraken Sport & Media published the *Manchester United Opus*, an epic book of giant proportions. Here are some *Opus* stats:

Weight: 37kg
Pages: 850, each measuring 50cm square
Content: 400,000 words and over 2,000 images
Price: £3,000 for Limited Edition of 9,500, each individually numbered from 501–10,000 and personally signed by Sir Alex Ferguson and Sir Bobby Charlton; £4,250 for Icons Edition, numbered 1–500 and additionally autographed by Eric Cantona, Bryan Robson and Denis Law

Many United players past and present purchased the *United Opu*s. Wayne Rooney bought number eight (before he changed his squad number to 10), David Beckham beat off stiff competition from other famous wearers of the seven shirt to the coveted copy number '7', while United's current occupant Cristiano Ronaldo plumped for '777'.

— UNDER LIGHTS —

The first game played under the Old Trafford lights was against Bolton Wanderers on March 23rd 1956. United wore an all red strip, as they were soon to play Real Madrid under the lights in the European Cup semi-final, and wanted to give the kit they would wear a practice run.

— CROSSING THE DIVIDE —

A list of players who have played for both United and Liverpool:

Liverpool to United:
Tom Miller (September 1920)
Tommy Reid (February 1929)
Ted Savage (January 1938)
Allenby Chilton (November 1938)

United to Liverpool:
John Sheldon (November 1913)
Fred Hopkin (May 1921)
Tommy McNulty (February 1954)
Phil Chisnall (April 1964)

— FERGIE'S BEST —

In 2006, more than 50,000 fans took part in a ManUtd.com poll to find Sir Alex Ferguson's best United side. They voted:

1. Treble winners 1999	61.7%
2. Double winners 1996	22.7%
3. Double winners 1994	9.3%
4. Champions 2003	4.6%
5. Cup Winners' Cup winners 1991	1.7%

— GOALSCORING GOALKEEPERS —

Goals scored by United goalkeepers:

Goalkeeper/match	Date	Competition
Alex Stepney v Leicester City*	September 12th 1973	Division One
Alex Stepney v Birmingham City*	October 20th 1973	Division One
Peter Schmeichel v Rotor Volgograd	September 26th 1995	UEFA Cup

* Penalty

— GEORDIE REDS XI —

Player	Born
Ray Wood (1949–59)	Hebburn-on-Tyne
Charlie Roberts (1905–13)	Darlington
Gary Pallister (1989–98)	Ramsgate, Kent but moved to the north-east as a child
Steve Bruce (1987–96)	Cornbridge, Northumberland
Bobby Charlton (1959–73)	Ashington, Northumberland
Jack Wilson (1926–32)	Leadgate, near Newcastle
Michael Carrick (2006–)	Wallsend
Bryan Robson (1981–94)	Chester-Le-Street, County Durham
George Wall (1906–15)	Boldon Colliery, County Durham
Joe Spence (1919–33)	Throckley, near Newcastle
Tom Smith (1923–27)	Whitburn, near Sunderland
Manager: Herbert Bamlett (1927–31)	Gateshead

— 'MOURINHO, ARE YOU LISTENING?' —

The white Pele

A selection of brilliant United songs:

"I saw my mate, the other day,
He said have you seen, the white Pele?
So I asked, who is he?
He goes by the name of Wayne Rooney,
Wayne Rooney, Wayne Rooney, He goes by the name of Wayne
Rooney"

"Mourinho are you listening?
Will you keep our trophy glistening?
We'll back in back in May,
To take it away,
Walking in a Fergie Wonderland"

"He plays on the left, [swing your arms to the left]
He plays on the riiiigggghhhhttt, [swing arms to the right]
The boy Ronaldo, makes England look s**te"

'*Park, Park, wherever you may be,*
You eat dog in your own country,
But it could be worse,
You could be Scouse,
Eating rat in your council house"
(**To the tune of 'The Lord of the Dance'**)

"Forever and ever,
We'll follow the boys,
Of Manchester United,
The Busby Babes,
For we made a promise,
To defend our faith,
In Manchester United,
The Busby Babes,
We've sworn allegiance,
To fight 'till we die,
To stand by United,
And the red flag we fly,
There'll be no surrender,
We'll fight to the last,
To defeat all before us,
As we did in the past,
For we're Stretford Enders,
With United we grew,
To the famous Red Devils,
We're loyal and true,
To part-time supporters,
We'll never descend,
We'll never forsake you,
We'll be here to the end,
For all we remember,
That '58 day,
And the plane that once stood on,
The Munich runway,
For the third fatal time,
The immortal young babes were,
Cut down in their prime,

In the cold snow of Munich,
They laid down their lives,
But they live on forever,
In our hearts and our minds,
Their names are now legend,
For the whole world to see,
Why this club's a religion,
Spelt M-U-F-C,
So bow down before them,
And lift up your eyes,
For Old Trafford's glory,
Will always survive . . ."
(**To the tune of 'Forever and Ever'**)

— HEATHENS UNDER FIRE —

In their first season in the Football League, 1892/93, Newton Heath conceded 30 goals in six consecutive games between January 2nd and March 4th 1893.

— ONE TO ELEVEN —

Since the introduction of squad numbers in 1993/94, United have only fielded numbers 1–11 from the start of a Premiership match on two occasions. This numerical oddity happened in successive games away to Sheffield United and away to Newcastle in December 1993. The team was:

1. Peter Schmeichel
2. Paul Parker
3. Dennis Irwin
4. Steve Bruce
5. Lee Sharpe
6. Gary Pallister
7. Eric Cantona
8. Paul Ince
9. Brian McClair
10. Mark Hughes
11. Ryan Giggs.

— CLOSE, BUT NOT CLOSE ENOUGH —

United finished runners-up in the old Football League First Division a total of nine times and have come close, but not close enough, in the Premiership on three occasions. United's points total of 88 in 1994/95 is the highest ever accumulated by a team which was not awarded the title.

Season	Second (points)	Champions (points)
1946/47	United (56)	Liverpool (57)
1947/48	United (52)	Arsenal (59)
1948/49	United (53)	Portsmouth (58)
1950/51	United (56)	Tottenham Hotspur (60)
1963/64	United (53)	Liverpool (57)
1967/68	United (56)	Manchester City (58)
1979/80	United (58)	Liverpool (60)
1987/88	United (81)	Liverpool (90)
1991/92	United (78)	Leeds (82)
1994/95*	United (88)	Blackburn (89)
1997/98*	United (77)	Arsenal (78)
2005/06*	United (83)	Chelsea (91)

*Premiership seasons

— ALL ROUNDERS —

Reds who excelled in other sports:

Kevin Moran	Gaelic footballer, played in two All Ireland finals
Arnie Sidebottom	Represented England at cricket in the 1985 Ashes series
Phil Neville	On the books of Lancashire Cricket Club and captained an England U-16 team that included Andrew Flintoff.
Thomas Wilcox	United keeper (1908–09) won the World Punchball (a form of baseball) Championship in the USA

— THE FLOWERS OF MANCHESTER —

*Aged just 21, Duncan Edwards had already made 175 appearances
for United before he died at Munich*

The Busby Babes who died in the 1958 Munich Air Disaster:

Duncan Edwards: Half-back, aged 21, 175 United appearances,
21 goals; 18 England caps, 5 goals

Liam 'Billy' Whelan: Forward, aged 22, 96 United appearances,
52 goals; 4 Ireland caps

Tommy Taylor: Forward, aged 26, 189 United appearances, 128 goals:
19 England caps, 6 goals

Roger Byrne: Full-back, aged 28, 277 United appearances; 19 goals,
33 England caps

Eddie Colman: Half-back, aged 21, 107 United appearances, 2 goals

David Pegg: Forward, aged 22, 148 United appearances, 28 goals;
1 England cap

Geoff Bent: Full-back, aged 25, 12 United appearances

Mark Jones: Half-back, aged 24, 120 United appearances, 1 goal

— THE ELITE FEW —

United skippers to have lifted the championship or Premier League trophies:

Charlie Roberts	1908, 1911
Johnny Carey	1952
Roger Byrne	1956, 1957
Denis Law	1965
Bobby Charlton	1967
Steve Bruce	1993, 1994, 1996
Eric Cantona	1997
Roy Keane	1999, 2000, 2001, 2003
Ryan Giggs/Gary Neville	2007

— OUCH THAT HURT —

United's biggest defeats *:

Football League	0–7 v Blackburn, April 10th 1926, Ewood Park
	0–7 v Aston Villa, December 27th 1930, Villa Park
	0–7 v Wolves, December 26th 1931, Molineux
Premiership	0–5 v Newcastle, October 20th 1996, St James' Park
	0–5 v Chelsea, October 3rd 1999, Stamford Bridge
FA Cup	1–7 v Burnley (first round replay), February 13th 1901, Turf Moor
League Cup	1–5 v Blackpool (second round), September 14th 1966, Bloomfield Road
Charity Shield	0–4 v Everton, August 17th 1963, Goodison Park
European Cup	0–4 v Milan (Semi-final second leg), May 14th 1958, San Siro
Champions League	0–4 v Barcelona (Group stage), November 2nd 1994, Camp Nou
UEFA/Fairs Cup	0–3 v Juventus (second round, second leg), November 3rd 1976, Stadio Communale
Cup Winners' Cup	0–5 v Sporting Lisbon (Quarter-final second leg), March 18th 1964, Estadio Jose Alvalade

* By margin of scoreline.

— PATRICE AND PATRICIA —

Patrice Evra's wife is called Patricia. The attacking full-back was born in Dakar, Senegal and is the son of a diplomat who moved to Europe when Patrice was a boy Evra's childhood friend was Thierry Henry and he was known as the 'Black Gazelle' by fans of Marsala, the Italian Serie C1 team based in Sicily with whom he first turned professional in 1998, aged just 17.

— UNBEATABLE —

United's longest ever run without losing a competitive match was between December 26th 1998 and September 25th 1999. The Reds went 45 games unbeaten, including 29 Premier League matches, eight in the FA Cup and eight in the Champions League. The run came to an end with a 5–0 Premiership defeat to Chelsea at Stamford Bridge.

— WEMBLEY '77 —

Some banners on display at the Jubilee Cup final in 1977 between United and Liverpool

'United We Are, United We Stand, The Greatest By Far, The Best In The Land, Manchester United'
'Watch Out Watch Out, There's a Greenhoff About'
'Jesus Saves, Stuart Pearson Nets The Rebound'
'I'd rather Be a Muppet Than a Scouse'
'Doc Scoops The "Pool"'
'Man United – 11 Wonders of The World'
'Doc's Red Army Walks On The Mersey'
'Doc's Jubilee – Wembley 1977'
'The Kop will topple to Hill and Coppell'

— LEAGUE CUP LAUNCHPAD —

Five players who made their United debut in League Cup ties:

Arthur Albiston	v Manchester City (h) October 9th 1974
Bryan Robson	v Tottenham (a) October 7th 1981
Mark Hughes	v Oxford (a) November 30th 1983
David Beckham	v Brighton (a) September 23rd 1992
Paul Scholes	v Port Vale (a) September 21st 1994

— WHERE ARE YOU WHEN WE ARE HERE? —

The 10 lowest post-war crowds to watch United in competitive fixtures:

Match	Date	Attendance
1. Bradford City, Valley Parade (League Cup)	November 2nd 1960	4,670
2. Burton Albion, Pirelli Stadium (FA Cup)	January 8th 2006	6,191
3. Djurgardens, Olympiastadion (Fairs Cup)	September 23rd 1964	6,537
4. Halifax Town, The Shay (League Cup)	September 26th 1990	6,841
5. Northampton Town, Sixfields (FA Cup)	January 25th 2004	7,356
6. LKS Lodz, LKS Stadium (Champions League)	August 26th 1998	8,000
7. Stoke City, Maine Road (Division One)	February 5th 1947	8,456
8. Oxford United, Manor Ground (Division One)	May 2nd 1988	8,966
9. Exeter City, St James' Park (FA Cup)	January 19th 2005	9,033
10. Luton Town, Kenilworth Road (Division One)	October 3rd 1987	9,137

— MASTERS OF THE UNIVERSE —

Players who have represented United's over-35s 'Masters' six-a-side team:

Chris Turner
Viv Anderson
Arthur Albiston
Mike Duxbury
Alan McLoughlin
Micky Thomas
Bryan Robson
Sammy McIlroy
Clayton Blackmore
Brian McClair

— RED STALWARTS —

Sir Bobby, 759 games for United

The all-time top 15 appearance holders in competitive games for United:

1.	Sir Bobby Charlton	1956–7	759
2.	Ryan Giggs	1990–	714*
3.	Bill Foulkes	1952–69	688
4.	Gary Neville	1992–	540*
5.	Alex Stepney	1966–78	540
6.	Tony Dunne	1960–73	539
7.	Paul Scholes	1992–	535*
8.	Denis Irwin	1991–2003	529
9.	Joe Spence	1919–33	510
10.	Arthur Albiston	1974–88	485
11.	Roy Keane	1993–2005	480

12	Brian McClair	1987–98	468
13.	George Best	1963–74	470
14.	Mark Hughes	1983–95	468
15.	Bryan Robson	1981–94	461

* Up to the end of the 2006/07 season

— LEAP OF FAITH —

United have played on February 29th just seven times:

Year	Competition	Result
1896	Division Two	1–2 v Burton Wanderers (h)
1908	Division One	1–0 v Birmingham City (h)
1912	FA Cup	3–0 v Reading (h)
1936	Division Two	3–2 v Blackpool (h)
1964	FA Cup	3–3 v Sunderland (h)
1972	FA Cup	3–0 v Middlesbrough (a)
1992	Division One	0–0 v Coventry City (a)

— CORK CONNECTION —

Reds who hailed from Cork, Ireland:

Noel Cantwell
Brian Carey
Denis Irwin
Roy Keane
Liam Miller
Frank O'Farrell (Manager 1971–72)

— FOOTBALLER OF THE YEAR —

Only six United players have ever been named Footballer of the Year. They are:

Johnny Carey	1949
Bobby Charlton	1966
George Best	1968
Eric Cantona	1996
Roy Keane	2000
Teddy Sheringham	2001
Cristiano Ronaldo	2007

– MUSIC FOR MUNICH –

'The Flowers of Manchester' was originally recorded by The Spinners in 1962. The sleeve notes state: "This wonderful tragic ballad was published anonymously in *Sing* magazine and set to Ewan MacColl's tune for 'The Ballad of John Axon'. It tells the story of the Munich Air Disaster in 1958 in which several of the Manchester United football team and their party were killed."

The Spinners were a folk group based in Liverpool, though one of their members, Mick Groves, who set the poem to a Ewan MacColl tune, was a Salford lad. For many years the songwriter was always written as 'Anonymous', but the words were actually written by Eric Winter, a journalist.

One cold and bitter Thursday, in Munich, Germany,
Eight great football stalwarts conceded victory,
Eight men will never play again, who met destruction there,
The flowers of English football, the flowers of Manchester.

Matt Busby's boys were flying returning from Belgrade,
This great United family, all masters of their trade,
The pilot of the aircraft, the skipper captain Thain,
Three times they tried to take off and twice turned back again.

The third time down the runway disaster followed close,
There was slush upon that runway and the aircraft never rose,
It ploughed into the marshy ground, it broke it overturned,
And eight of that team were killed when the blazing wreckage
    burned.

Roger Byrne and Tommy Taylor who were capped for England's
    side,
And Ireland's Billy Whelan and England's Geoff Bent died.

Mark Jones and Eddie Colman and David Pegg also,
They all lost their lives as it ploughed on through the snow.

Big Duncan went too, with an injury to his frame,
And Ireland's brave Jack Blanchflower will never play again.
The great Matt Busby lay there, the father of this team,
Three long months passed by before he saw his team again.

The trainer, coach and secretary and a member of the crew,
Eight great sporting journalists with who United flew,
And one of them was Big Swifty who we will ne'er forget,
The finest English keeper, that ever graced a net.

Oh England's finest football team its record truly great,
Its proud successes mocked by a twist of fate,
Eight met who'll never play again who met destruction there,
The Flowers of English football, the Flowers of Manchester.'

— TREBLE WINNERS —

Only four European sides have completed the treble of domestic league and cup and the European Cup/Champions League in the same season. They are:

Celtic	1967
Ajax	1972
PSV Eindhoven	1988
Manchester United	**1999**

— HOME SWEET HOME —

United's home grounds:

- **North Road** (Monsall) 1878–93: Newton Heath's first stadium.
- **Bank Street** (Clayton) 1893–1910): Despite a 50,000 capacity and what was England's first covered stand, was deemed 'too small' for United.
- **Old Trafford** (1910–present)

Temporary homes:

- **Maine Road** (Moss Side) 1945–49: United paid Manchester City £5,000 per match to use their ground after Old Trafford was bombed in the Second World War.
- **Goodison Park** (Liverpool) and **Leeds Road** (Huddersfield): Used for FA Cup third and fourth round ties in 1947/48 because City were playing at Maine Road.
- **Anfield** (Liverpool) and the **Victoria Ground** (Stoke): Used for league games in 1971/72 when United were banned from playing at home due to crowd trouble.
- **Home Park** (Plymouth): Hosted a UEFA Cup tie with St Etienne in 1977 after United were banned from using Old Trafford following crowd trouble at the away leg.

— SILVER SERVICE —

United's 11 most decorated players, by winners' medals won:

	League	FA Cup	Lge Cup	Euro Cup	ECWC	Super Cup	Inter	Total
Ryan Giggs	9	3	2	1	–	1	1	17
Denis Irwin	7	2	1	1	1	1	1	14
Gary Neville	7	3	1	1	–	–	1	13
Paul Scholes	7	3	1	1	–	–	1	13
Roy Keane	7	3	–	1	–	–	1	12
Phil Neville	6	3	–	1	–	–	1	11
Peter Schmeichel	5	3	1	1	–	1	–	11
Nicky Butt	6	3	–	1	–	–	1	11
Ole Solskjaer	6	2	1	1	–	–	1	11
Gary Pallister	4	3	1	–	1	1	–	10
David Beckham	6	2	–	1	–	–	1	10
Managers:								
Alex Ferguson	9	5	2	1	1	1	1	20
Matt Busby	5	2	–	1	–	–	–	8
Ernest Mangnall	2	1	–	–	–	–	–	3

*Not including the Charity Shield or Community Shield

— LET THERE BE LIGHT —

The first floodlit game in Manchester was on February 26th 1889 when Newton Heath played Ardwick (an early incarnation of Manchester City) at Belle Vue Gardens in a charity match that raised £140 for victims of an explosion at Hyde Colliery. Old Trafford's floodlights were first used on March 25th 1957 when a crowd 60,862 watched United lose 2–0 to Bolton Wanderers.

— ARE YOU BEING SERBED? —

Nemanja Vidic was part of the Serbian and Montenegrin national team's 'Famous Four' defence, alongside Mladen Krstajic, Ivica Dragutinovic and Goran Gavrancic. The quartet conceded just one goal during the ten 2006 FIFA World Cup qualification matches, the best defensive record of any of the qualifying teams.

Then they went and lost 6–0 to Argentina in the finals!

— RED FLOPS —

Ten big money signings who failed to cut the mustard at Old Trafford:

Gary Birtles: Recycled jokes no. 65. "The first thing American hostages asked when released from Iran in 1981 was 'Has Birtles scored yet?'" The joke was valid as the £1.25m club record signing from Forest played 25 games in his first season . . . and didn't score once. He was sold back to Forest for £275,000 less than two years later, his 12 goals in 64 appearances poor value.

Ralph Milne: Still portrayed as a tragic comedy figure by United fans, Milne was a decent winger with Dundee United. He then found his level playing with Second Division Bristol City . . . before Sir Alex swooped like an eagle chasing a wild rabbit.

Diego Forlan: Forlan's Birtles-esque start to a United career stuck with him and for £7m, United fans expected more than 10 goals in 62 matches. Now scoring for fun in Spain having moved from Villarreal to Athletico Madrid. It was always going to happen.

Juan Sebastian Veron: Outstanding in some games (usually European ones), anonymous in others. Reds were not unreasonable to hope for more for £28.1m. Now playing back in Argentina.

Colin Gibson: The ultra fit left back who played in the Aston Villa side which won the league and European Cup. It wasn't his fault his time at United didn't work out – the club's doctors never diagnosed his cruciate injury. Leicester's did . . .

Nicola Jovanovic: United's first foreign signing in 1980. He came, he saw and he buggered off back to Belgrade after 25 games . . . along with his club BMW.

Eric Djemba Djemba: He was intended to replace Roy Keane. They cost the same. That's where comparisons end.

Neil Webb: Classy after signing from Forest in 1989. Less than spectacular after picking up an injury on international duty a month after becoming a Red. Cruelly exposed by the *Sun* for the heinous crime of being a postman.

Terry Gibson: The moustachioed, Pot-Noodle sized striker cost £630,000 in 1986 and scored once before leaving for Wimbledon for £200,000. Do the maths: £430,000 for one goal.

Ted MacDougall: An expensive panic buy from Bournemouth in September 1972, the words: "United" and "Not good enough to play for" abounded as he slunk south to West Ham five months later.

— THE OTHER WAR OF THE ROSES —

A brief history of the longstanding enmity between the Uniteds of Lancashire and Yorkshire:

- Ill feeling prevailed when United's skilful young Irish winger Johnny Giles fell out with Matt Busby and moved to Elland Road in 1963. In 1965 United reached their fourth consecutive FA Cup semi-final where they met Leeds. Both clubs were battling for success in the league and cup – literally. In front of 65,000 at Hillsborough, Jack Charlton and Denis Law wrestled like two schoolboys as players swapped punches. The game finished 0–0, with the referee, both managers and players all being criticised for their conduct.

- The replay was in Nottingham four days later where players fought again. Rival fans followed, with one running on the pitch and knocking the referee to the ground, and there were disturbances on the terraces with stories of fans being thrown into the River Trent confirmed by police. Leeds won the tie 1–0 with a last-minute Billy Bremner goal set up by, yes, Johnny Giles. Still, United finished the season as champions for the first time in eight years – on goal difference from Leeds.

- Busby's third side peaked with 1968 European Cup success. Leeds, meanwhile, consistently won major honours. In 1970, an aging United team drew Leeds in the FA Cup semi-final. "The game was spoiled by the weather," recalls Johnny Giles of the 0–0 draw at Hillsborough.

- "The second game at Villa Park was in the top three that I ever played in," adds Giles. "There were no goals, but there was passion, great players and skill. It had everything except goals."

- 173,500 people had watched the tie by the time Leeds won the third game at Burnden Park, 1–0. "All the players were tired after three games in less than a week," concludes Giles.

- On 19th February 1972, Leeds hammered United 5–1 at Elland Road. Relegated in 1974, Leeds fans greeted the United team upon their return a year later with the song: "Where were you in '74?" Playing great football to capacity crowds, actually.

- The pair were drawn together in a 1977 FA Cup semi-final at Hillsborough and both teams were allocated 21,000 tickets with Sheffield Wednesday receiving the 'neutral' 13,000. After United's allocation sold out, Mancunian touts bought up many of these tickets and with Leeds not selling their allocation, one newspaper described the scene: "Within 15 minutes Manchester United were two-up, delighting a crowd in which the red of Lancashire so dominated the yellow and white of Yorkshire that Hillsborough looked like an egg with a whole bottle of tomato ketchup poured over it." United won 2–1 and went on to lift the cup.

- Leeds fans were stunned in 1978 when, over a three-week period, they lost their best two players, Gordon McQueen and Joe Jordan, for record fees . . . to Manchester United. It wasn't until the following season that the pair had to face their old club wearing the red shirts. The insults flew, but seven minutes into the game United were awarded a corner at the Gelderd End. As McQueen moved forward the abuse got louder and by the time he reached the penalty area missiles were being thrown. McQueen's subsequent header and goal stunned the home fans.

- Leeds were relegated in 1982 and tales of the 60s and 70s rivalry were passed down to younger fans. They returned to the top flight with Howard Wilkinson in 1990 and in a 17-day period over December 1991 and January 1992, played United three times at Elland Road – first in the league then in the League Cup and finally in the FA Cup. United won both the cup ties and drew the league game, but red smugness evaporated months later when Leeds, free to concentrate on the league, held their nerve and piped United to the title. In the public celebrations, Eric Cantona muttered: "I don't know why. But I love you". We'll forget about that.

- In 1999 United returned from a gruelling 3–3 game in Barcelona to face a talented young Leeds side who had lost just one of their first 14 league games. It was two after United won 3–2.

- With a strong young squad managed by David O'Leary, Leeds topped the table when United visited in February 2000. Andrew Cole's superb solo goal brought United victory and provided the impetus for a sixth championship in eight years. Within weeks, United fans noted the significance of the victory by singing: "We Won the League At Elland Road."

- United last played Leeds in the 2003/04 season, drawing 1–1 at Old Trafford and winning 1–0 at Elland Road. Following the Yorkshire side's relegation to the third tier of English football at the end of 2006/07 it could be some time before the paths of the two Uniteds cross again.

— TEAMS WE LOVE TO HATE —

Liverpool: The eternal rivals. It's about time they started playing their part in the billing in the league. Actually, no it's not.

City: Deluded neighbours who don't win trophies.

Arsenal: More a football rivalry rather than one born out of mutual loathing. It's not like fans from the Emirates library wind us up is it?

Leeds United: "We all hate Leeds scum." Reds sing it for a reason . . .

Bolton Wanderers: Belligerent, moustachioed, pie-eating yonners.

Chelsea: The plastic club for mercenaries and tourists. Chart climbers. Average crowds were 21,000 a decade ago.

Aston Villa: Given the number of empty seats at Villa Park when United don't visit, a classic case of, "You've only come to see United."

Galatasaray: Old wounds run deep for their appalling treatment of United's players and fans in the mid-90s.

Newcastle: Overweight, indecipherable fans who get married in their replica shirts and shout 'Toon' at their black and white dogs. Which may or not be their wife in that part of the world.

— MANCUNIAN LANDMARKS WITH UNITED LINKS —

1. Eddie Colman Court, Salford

Ordsal boy Colman was a Busby Babe who perished at Munich. His name is dedicated to a Salford tower block, now used as student accommodation by the University of Salford.

2. Davyhulme Park Golf Club

Before a gradual shift to the south of the city, Davyhulme was home to several United players in the 1950s and 1960s. The players met in Davyhulme's art deco clubhouse five miles west of Old Trafford for a pre-match steak.

3. Mottram Hall

Visiting European teams now usually stay at the Worsley Marriot rather than Mottram Hall, but the Cheshire hotel was where Sir Alex learned that United were the champions of England in 1993 whilst having a round of golf. He joyfully passed on the good news to a fellow golfer, a Japanese chap with 'Sharp', United's then sponsors, emblazoned on his jacket. The Japanese guy didn't know what he was on about.

4. The Imperial Hotel
Not only were the PFA formed at a meeting in the Imperial Hotel, the name Manchester United was decided there on April 26th 1902. Manchester Central and Manchester Celtic were dismissed, the former because it sounded too much like a railway station, but director Louis Rocca allegedly proposed the name Manchester United. The hotel, close to Piccadilly Station, stood as a public house until the 1990s before being demolished to make way for the Malmaison Hotel.

5. Albert Square.
Manchester is not noted for its open public spaces, but the town hall balcony overlooking the square was the destination for many a victorious Red homecoming parade. Safety concerns mean it is no longer used to show off new silverware. That decision, taken 20 years ago, has yet to affect City.

6. George Best's old house, near Bramhall
Best referred to his newly commissioned ultra-modern house as his 'Saturn Five Space Station House'. Fans besieged it in the early 1970s and played football on the lawn outside. Architectural critics claimed it looked like a lavatory from the outside. Inside, the lavish furnishings consisted of the copious use of marble, full-length tinted windows . . . and plenty of female visitors.

7. The Cliff, Lower Broughton, Salford
The Cliff was United's main training ground until the move to Carrington in 2000. It was used as a home for the United ladies and girls teams until the former became defunct. It is now the main base for the Under-9 and Under-10 academy teams.

— SOUTH AMERICAN REDS —

Only five Latin Americans have worn United red:

Diego Forlan (Uruguay)
Juan Sebastian Veron (Argentina)
Kleberson (Brazil)
Gabriel Heinze (Argentina)
Anderson (Brazil)

— FATAL APPEARANCES —

- Thomas Blackstock, who made a total of 38 first team appearances, died while playing for United against St Helens Recs in a Lancashire Combination fixture in April 1907. In the opening minutes of the game, he headed the ball out for a throw-in, before collapsing. He was carried from the pitch and died in the dressing room.
- In another Lancashire Combination match between Newton Heath reserves and Darwen reserves on October 19th 1892, Darwen forward Joseph Aspden was involved in an accidental collision with James Brown. Aspden was carried off the pitch but returned home. He died four days later after collapsing. In the subsequent inquest, Brown told how he had slipped, catching Aspden in the stomach with his knee.

— MORE GREAT FLAGS —

'Joe Royle's Fat Head': Reds in Valencia in 2000 offered their appreciation of the incredibly large cranium of the then City boss.

'Atkinson's Long Leather': Fair play to Liverpool fans for picking up on the sartorial faux pas of the then United manager. What did they expect from a fellow Scouser?

'We all know that Manchester Is Red': Just how did United fans get a similar flag into City's Kippax Stand in 2002? Better still, how did they get City fans to pass it above their heads?

'17 Years': The original banner which pointed out the number of years since City won a trophy. First spotted in Budapest in 1993. An updated version now adorns the Stretford End.

'MUFC The Religion': Another current Stretford End reworking.

'MUFC – We're Too Sexy For Milan': The San Siro, 1999.

'Feb 6th 1958 – The Flowers of Manchester': Found its rightful home on the Stretford End.

Big Lily: That's the name of the giant red, white and black flag owned by Carrickfergus Red Keith.

'Buchan Defender Of The Faith': He was. Spotted at Wembley 1977.

'Play Up United – Give It To Joe.': A banner for 1919–1933 star Joe Spence.

— HOLA! —

A selection of Reds who have lived in sunny Spain:

Stuart Pearson: Pancho lives near Alicante. He still returns for home games to do corporate hospitality.

Brian Greenhoff: Menorca is now the home to the 1970s United defender.

John Gidman: The raffish 1980s right back lives near Marbella.

Ashley Grimes: United's mop-haired 80's midfielder ran with the bulls of Osasuna in Pamplona for two years.

Mark Hughes: Left for Barca in 1986. His Spanish didn't get past the 'dos cervezas' stage. Perhaps he learnt Catalan . . .

Kevin Moran: The only man to be sent off in an FA Cup final left United for Sporting Gijon in evergreen Asturias.

Peter Barnes: The son of the man who scouted Giggs for City spent a year baking in Seville with Real Betis.

Diego Forlan: Profligacy pays . . . Forlan got a pay rise when he joined Villarreal.

Quinton Fortune: When he told his team-mates in Atletico Madrid's reserve team that he was joining Manchester United they thought he was joking.

David Beckham: Played for four years for a team called Real Madrid. You didn't know?

— THE 10 MOST EXPENSIVE UNITED AWAY TICKETS —

1. Porto 2003/04: £65
2. Juventus 1998/99: £56
3. Shanghai 1999/00: £55
3. AC Milan in New York 2004/05: £55
5. Olympiakos 2002/03: £52
6. Chelsea 2003/04: £49
7. Arsenal 2006/07: £46
8. Birmingham City 2004/05: £45
8. Fulham 2006/07: £45
10. The average ticket price at Old Trafford in 2004/05 was £26.50 and the average price to watch the 1999 Champions League final was just £21.

— WHEN THE SEAGULLS . . .
MORE ERIC QUOTES —

"I imagine the ball to be alive, sensitive, responding to the touch of my foot, to my caresses, like a woman with the man she loves."

"I only know one way to take penalties: to score them."

"In the modern game of football there are great musicians, but Glenn Hoddle is like Mozart among the hard rock men."

"An artist, in my eyes, is someone who can lighten up a dark room. I have never, and never will, find any difference between the pass from Pele to Carlos Alberto in the final of the World Cup in 1970 and the poetry of young Rimbaud. There is, in each of these human manifestations, an expression of beauty which touches us and gives us a feeling of eternity."

"I leave when I need to change. It's like being with a woman. If you get to the point when you've got nothing left to say to her, you leave. Or else you stop being good."

"In Manchester the public is faithful, married for eternity to its players."

"In England everything is beautiful. The stadiums are beautiful, the atmosphere is beautiful, the cops on horseback are beautiful. The crowds respect you."

"I value truth, honesty, respect for one another, compassion and understanding. I have found these qualities in Manchester United."

"I've been punished for striking a goalkeeper. For spitting at supporters. For throwing my shirt at a referee. For calling my manager a bag of shit. I called those who judged a bunch of idiots. I thought I might have trouble finding a sponsor."

"To achieve happiness you sometimes have to go through the worst depths of despair."

"I have played professional football for 13 years, which is a long time. I now wish to do other things. I have always planned to retire at the top, and at Manchester United I have reached the pinnacle of my career."

— VETERAN REDS —

The oldest players to appear for United are:

Player	Age	Year
1. Bill Meredith	46 years, 281 days	1921
2. Raimond van der Gouw	39 years, 48 days	2002
3. Frank Mann	38 years, 240 days	1929
4. Jack Warner	38 years, 213 days	1950
5. Thomas Jones	38 years, 5 days	1937
6. Teddy Partridge	37 years, 323 days	1929
7. George Livingstone	37 years, 313 days	1914
8. Clarence Hilditch	37 years, 243 days	1932
9. Bill Foulkes	37 years, 223 days	1969
10. Bryan Robson	37 years, 117 days	1994

— LOCAL LADS —

Players born within spitting distance of Old Trafford:

Brian Kidd and Nobby Stiles: Collyhurst lads who went to the same school. Kidd lives in Middleton and was frequently spotting training in a United tracksuit top whilst assistant manager at Leeds. Stiles lives in Stretford.

Remi Moses: One of the few black kids to grow up in Miles Platting's school of hard knocks resulted in a very, very hard player.

Phil Chisnall: The last player to transfer between United and Liverpool, over 40 years ago, is from Stretford. He now lives in Urmston and works in a malt loaf factory.

Paul Scholes: From the Langley Estate, near Middleton, where Ken Loach set his film *Raining Stones*.

Shay Brennan: The 'Irishman' who made the goal that won the 1968 European Cup was born in Manchester.

Roger Byrne: The great captain of the Busby's Babes was born in Gorton, died in Munich and is buried in Stretford.

Nicky Butt: Gorton's most recent finest.

Denis Viollet: Prolific goalscorer who grew up in Moss Side and supported City as a kid.

Wes Brown: Longsight lad. As Manc as the Co-Op Bank.

Eddie Colman, Geoff Bent: Both Salford born and bred. Both lost at Munich.

John Aston senior and junior: The father and son who played for United.

— OLD TRAFFORD FAN STEREOTYPES —

1. The Old Timer

Most likely to say: "He's not a patch on Billy Meredith*/Johnny Carey*/Duncan Edwards*/Best – Law – Charlton*". *Delete according to age.

Least likely to say: "They don't get paid enough, the players of today."

2. The Day Tripper

Most likely to say: "It's a Ronaldo corner. Get the camera out."

Least likely to say: "You applied for Everton away yet?"

3. The Singer

Most likely to say (whilst gesticulating wildly): "Come on! Sing!"

Least likely to say: "Quiet please, my concentration has been known to lapse due to noise during play."

4. The Away Fan

Most likely to say: Who cares?

Least likely to say: "Credit where it's due, it's a wonderful stadium and United are a cracking team."

5. Family Stand Parent

Most likely to say (to child): "Of course you can keep the ball if it comes over here and you catch it."

Least likely to say (to child five minutes into the second half): "Of course I'd love to escort you to the toilet for the fourth time."

6. The Executive Fan

Most likely to say (the visiting client, that is): "That Ryan Ronaldo's having a good game up front. You were saying that he was going out with that Canadian supermodel – Hillary Clinton".

Least likely to say: "The second half has just started and the bar is empty."

7. The Hooligan

Most likely to say: "They had 40 at Piccadilly before the game."

Least likely to say: "I'll be buying one of those jester hats after the match."

8. The Disabled fan

Most likely to say: "We can enjoy the game in peace now Niall Quinn has retired."

Least likely to say: "The facilities at Old Trafford are worse than at other clubs."

9. The Drunk

Most likely to say: "Shall we go down for a half-time pint ten minutes before the break?"

Least likely to say: "Their tactical awareness has to be noted."

10. The Footballer's Wife

Most likely to say: "What colours do United wear again?"

Least likely to say: "I won't bother with the players' lounge after the game."

11. The Every Gamer

Most likely to say: "How would you know – you weren't even at Videoton in '85?"

Least likely to say: "It's good to see so many Scandinavian faces in the United end at Anfield today."

— NOTABLE OLD TRAFFORD FIRSTS —

First match: February 19th 1910 v Liverpool (3–4) Att. 45,000

First FA Cup tie: February 4th 1911 v Aston Villa (2–1) Att. 65,101

First Football League Cup tie: October 26th 1960 v Exeter City (4–1) Att. 15,662

First European tie*: April 25th 1957 v Real Madrid (2–2) Att. 65,000

First victory: March 5th 1910 v Sheffield United (1–0) Att.40,000

First goal: February 19th 1910, Thomas Homer v Liverpool

First hat-trick: April 30th 1910 v Middlesbrough, John Picken scored four

* Earlier European Cup ties in the 1956/57 season were played at Maine Road as Old Trafford did not have floodlights

— THE BIG RED BOOK —

United people who have appeared on *This is Your Life*:

Bobby Charlton
Denis Law
George Best
Nobby Stiles
Bryan Robson
Matt Busby

— STALWARTS IN THE DUG-OUT —

The 11 longest-serving United managers are:

1. Sir Matt Busby (1945–1969 and 1970–71)
2. Sir Alex Fergsuon (1986–)
3. Ernest Mangnall (1903–1912)
4. Walter Crickmer (1931–1932 and 1937–1945)
5. John Robson (1914–1921)
6. Tommy Docherty (1972–77)
7. Scott Duncan (1932–37)
8. Ron Atkinson (1981–86)
9. John Chapman (1921–26)
10. Herbert Bamlett (1927–31)
11. Dave Sexton (1977–81)

— PALINDROMIC DATES —

United have only played on palindromic dates (dates that read the same forwards as they do backwards in DD/MM/YY format) twice. On November 11th 1911 (11/11/11) United drew 0–0 at home with Preston while on November 30th 2003 (30/11/03) the Reds lost 1–0 to Chelsea at Stamford Bridge.

— NOT SO TOP SCOTS —

Scottish teams below Premier League level that United have played in friendlies:

St Johnstone, Dumbarton, Queen of the South, Ross County, East Fife, Livingstone, Clyde, Dundee, Partick Thistle, Airdrie (now Airdrie United)

— FROM PITCH TO DUG-OUT —

United managers and assistant managers who also played for the club:

Sir Alex Ferguson (in a friendly), Wilf McGuinness, Lal Hilditch, Pat Crerand, Archie Knox, Brian Kidd, Mike Phelan, Tommy Docherty (in a friendly)

MAN UTD
Home Kits
1880-2009

www.historicalkits.co.uk

1880
(Newton Heath)

1892
(Newton Heath)

1892-93
(Newton Heath)

1894-95
(Newton Heath)

1895-1902
(Newton Heath)

1902-03

1908-09

1919-22

1922-26

1926-34

1934-35

1935-39

1946-47

1947-56

1956-59

1959-61

1961-65

1965-71

1971-72

1972-74

1974-75

1975-80

1980-82

1982-83

1983-84

1984-86

1986-88

1988-90

1990-92

1992-94

1994-96

1996-98

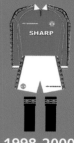

1998-2000

2000-02

2002-04

2004-06

2006-07

2007-09

— NEWTON HEATH FACTFILE —

- **Most appearances in Football League:** Fred Erentz, 280 between seasons 1892/93 and 1901/02.
- **Most goals in Football League:** Joe Cassidy, 91 in 152 games between seasons 1892/93 and 1900/01.
- **Most Football League goals in a season:** Henry Boyd, 20 in season 1897/98.
- **Best Football League position**: Bottom of Division One in seasons 1892/93 and 1893/94.
- **Best FA Cup performance:** Third round in season 1896/97 where they lost 2–0 to Derby County. It is worth noting that Newton Heath played seven games to reach this round, defeating West Manchester 7–0, Nelson 3–0, Blackpool 2–1 (after a 2–2 draw), Kettering Town 5–1 and Southampton 3–1 (after a 1–1draw).
- **Most league points:** 44 in Division Two in 1899/1900 from 34 games.
- **Most league goals:** 78 in season 1894/95.
- **Most league wins:** 20 in season 1899/1900.
- **Best league win:** 10–1 v Lincoln City on November 21st 1891 and 10–1 v Wolverhampton Wanderers on October 15th 1892.
- **Best FA Cup win:** 7–0 v West Manchester on December 12th 1896.
- **First league match:** Blackburn Rovers away on September 3rd 1892, lost 4–3.
- **First home league match:** Burnley on September 10th 1892, drew 1–1.
- **First FA Cup tie:** Fleetwood Rangers away on October 30th 1886, drew 2–2 (however, Newton Heath refused to play extra-time and the tie was awarded to Fleetwood).
- **First trophy won:** Manchester and District Cup in season 1885/86.
- **First recorded match:** v Bolton Wanderers X1 on November 20th 1880, lost 6–0.
- **Last recorded match**: v Manchester City on April 26th 1902 in the Manchester Senior Cup Final, won 2–1.

— ALL ACTION SMITHY —

As a youngster, former Reds striker Alan Smith was a keen BMX racer and at the age of eight was the British champion for his age. He chose to give that up in favour of playing football.

— THE WATNEY CUP —

Denis Law: The first player in England to miss in a penalty shoot-out

The Watney Mann Invitation Cup (normally referred to as simply the Watney Cup) was an early 1970s tournament. Held before the start of the season, it was contested by the teams that had scored the most goals in each of the four divisions of the Football League the previous season who had not been promoted or admitted to one of the European competitions.

Two teams from each division took part, making eight participants in total. The competition was a straight knockout format, with each match a one-off with no replays. The final took place at the home ground of one of the finalists, rather than a neutral venue. The competition's name came from a sponsorship deal with the Watney Mann brewery, one of the first such deals in English football. Watney Cup matches were also televised live which was a rare occurrence in the 1970s.

The tournament ran four times, from 1970 to 1973. After beating Reading and Hull away in front of near capacity crowds, United reached the final in the first competition in 1970. After a 1–1 draw after extra-time, the semi-final against Hull was decided by England's first ever penalty shoot-out. The first footballer to take a kick was George Best who scored, the first to miss Denis Law who missed United's fourth, but the Reds won the shoot-out 4–2. Their reward was a final at Derby County, which the they lost 4–1.

United played in the competition the following season, when Halifax Town produced a shock result to knock the Reds out after a 2–1 win.

— OLD FAVES —

Songs and chants that used to be part of the Stretford End's repertoire, but no longer:

'You'll Never Walk Alone'
'Your going to get your ******* head kicked in'
'You're going home in a St John's ambulance'
'You must have come in a taxi'
'I'd walk a million miles for one of your goals, oh Denis . . . '

— THE MUNICH CLOCK —

The Munich Clock is found on the outside of the south-east corner of Old Trafford. An understated clock, bearing the date of the tragedy – February 6th 1958 – many visiting fans believe the clock shows the exact time of the crash. In fact it is a working clock that shows the actual time.

— RED REFEREES —

Former Newton Heath players Herbert Dale and George Owen both went on to become referees.

Herbert Bamlett, United manager between 1927 and 1931, was the youngest referee to take charge of the FA Cup final – the 1914 final between Burnley and Liverpool. He was also the referee for the 1909 quarter-final tie between Burnley and United at Turf Moor which he abandoned with 18 minutes remaining and the home side winning 1–0. United won the re-arranged fixture 3–2.

John Bentley, United's secretary between 1912 and 1916, was also a top class referee.

— MEMBERSHIP FLOP —

When United's membership scheme was introduced in the summer of 1987, so few fans joined up that the members' only Stretford End was half empty for the first home game of the season against Arsenal. The 42,890 crowd was almost 10,000 down on the corresponding fixture the previous season.

— NEWTON HEATH MISCELLANY —

- None of the players who lined up for Newton Heath's first match in the Football Alliance on September 21st 1889 were present when the Heathens played their last match against City. Only F.C. Erentz and J. Coupar played in the first Football League match against Burnley and that last fixture against City. Fittingly, Erentz was one of the scorers against City.
- A local chimney-sweep known as 'Father' Bird was known to entertain Newton Heath players and officials at his home with a sing-song and a supper of either Lancashire hot-pot or potato pie.
- Mr Sedgwick, station master at Victoria Station, always made sure that the Heathens players travelled to away fixtures in luxury reserved coaches.
- While Fred the Red is a familiar figure walking round the Old Trafford pitch, at Bank Street they had a goose (the fabled 'Bank Street Canary') and a goat that was known on occasions to get drunk.
- The first floodlit match played at Clayton was a benefit match for Harry Stafford and Walter Cartwright against Manchester City. The game was played in a strong gale and the lights kept on blowing out. When only one lamp remained alight, the referee abandoned the match. On reaching the dressing-rooms, the referee discovered that half the players were already washed and changed.
- When gates were particularly low, players were paid according to attendances.
- Collections were often made between supporters in order to pay for transport to away fixtures, such was the poor state of affairs at the club.

— FRIENDS AND FOES —

Real Madrid were generous to United after the Munich air disaster, playing a series of friendly games. In October 1960, Madrid, who had won the first four European Cups, destroyed United 6–1 at Old Trafford. In the return game the following month United kept the score down to 6–5. Madrid appeared for half of their usual fee.

— BACK OF THE NET —

By late December 1973, United's top goalscorer was goalkeeper Alex Stepney with two goals. Stepney scored penalties against Birmingham and Leicester, but he missed from the spot in the 2–1 home defeat to Wolverhampton Wanderers. He'd also scored in a pre-season friendly shoot-out against Uruguayan side Penarol.

— THE GRASS IS GREENER . . . —

Players who did well after leaving Old Trafford:

- Alan McLaughlin left Old Trafford in 1986, without ever playing in the first team. He went on to play over 560 senior games with the likes of Swindon and Portsmouth, while also picking up 42 caps for the Republic of Ireland.
- David Platt was discarded by United in 1984, but went on to play for Crewe Alexandra, Aston Villa, Arsenal, Nottingham Forest and England, as well as having a successful spell in Italy, scoring over 200 goals in 585 appearances. He also scored 27 times in 62 England internationals.
- Frank Kopel made only 12 senior appearances with United, but made over 300 for Dundee United.
- John Scott appeared only three times for United but played 240 times for Grimsby Town.
- Peter O'Sullivan left United in 1970 as a 19-year-old never having played in the first team, but went on to play for Brighton, Fulham, Charlton, Reading and Aldershot, as well as in Hong Kong, making over 500 appearances in total (435 of them with Brighton). He was also capped by Wales.

— RED ON RED —

United's first team used to play the reserves at Old Trafford, with the two junior sides playing each other prior to this, as a pre-season curtain raiser. This was a chance for fans to see any new summer signings. These days, fans are invited to an open training session at Old Trafford.

— YER WOT? —

Some unusual United player names:

Alphonso Ainsworth
Beaumont Asquith
J. Ignatius Feehan
Caesar Augustus Llewelyn Jenkyns
Proctor Hall
Horace Elford Blew
Lancelot Holliday Richardson
Ole Gunnar Solskjaer
Arnoldus Johannus Hyacinthus Muhren

— WAR HEROES —

Oscar Linkson, Sandy Turnbull and Pat McGuire (an amateur reserve player) were all killed in action during the First World War.

Allenby Chilton made his United debut in 1939, the day before the Second World War broke out. He did not make his second appearance until seven years later. In the meantime, he enlisted in the Durham Light Infantry (he was born in County Durham) and was twice wounded, at Caen and during the D-Day landings. During the war, Chilton also helped assist Charlton Athletic to victory in the League Cup south final. In the end the rock-hard defender, who had once trained as a boxer, made 390 appearances for United. Imagine what that figure would have been had the war not taken seven years from his Old Trafford career?

Goalkeeper Reg Allen was signed from Queens Park Rangers in 1950. His £11,000 fee was the first five figure transfer for a goalkeeper and a world record for the position. Allen was a commando during the Second World War and was a former prisoner of war after being captured in North Africa.

— WE'LL BE BACK —

When Preston North End played United at Old Trafford in April 1958, their two wing-half backs were Tommy Docherty and Frank O'Farrell. The former replaced the latter as United manager in December 1972 and O'Farrell is also godfather to one of Docherty's sons.

— THE UNITED REVIEW —

Some facts about the Reds' matchday programme:

- In the first domestic post-war season, 1946/47, United's highest programme sales were 19,032 against Nottingham Forest in the FA Cup, 18,860 against Bolton Wanderers and 14,772 against Wolves. Their lowest sales were against Burnley and Preston North End in the Lancashire Cup, selling 1,074 and 2,316 respectively.
- The first post-war programme to include action photographs was against Sunderland on March 6th 1948 (no.17). The first time one appeared on the front cover was against Huddersfield Town on September 4th 1948 (no.3).
- The highest ever selling *United Review* was the one for the World Club Championship against Estudiantes in 1968, with an estimated 74,680 being sold.
- Programmes used to feature a 'token'. The idea was that fans would buy the programme as proof that they had attended the game. For big games where there was a limited ticket availability such as cup finals, tickets would be distributed first to fans with the most tokens. This first token appeared in season 1956/57, with the token sheet being printed on the back cover of the first issue of that season against Birmingham City. The last season in which it was included in the programme was 1991/92. Special tokens were given out three or four times per season to fans who also attended reserve or youth team games, but the system was open to manipulation and was dropped.
- The *United Review* was sold for the first time outside Old Trafford at the start of season 1993/94. That meant that even more fanzine sellers were asked: 'Is that the programme?'
- The player and spectator shaking hands logo on the *United Review* for the 1994/95 season was not computer generated but an actual photograph. The 'player' was David Ingram, who at that time was appearing in the *Rocky Horror Show* in London, while the 'supporter' was Danny Elkan, an actor who had appeared in the BBC series *Casualty*.

— HAS IT FINISHED YET? —

The longest fixture involving the club lasted 420 minutes – an intermediate FA Cup tie between Newton Heath and Small Heath (who became Birmingham City) in 1903/04. The tie went into four games, the first three being drawn 1–1 and two of them going to extra time. Newton Heath won the final game 3–1.

— SELLING UP —

Former defender Bill Foulkes, who is third on United's all-time appearance list behind Sir Bobby Charlton and Ryan Giggs, sold his 1968 European Cup winners medal for £12,100 at Christie's, Glasgow, in October 1992. His number five jersey from the game was also sold at the auction, for £1,980. Both figures include the 10 per cent sales premium.

— HOWZAT? —

3,045 fans attended a seven-a-side knockout floodlight cricket competition at United's Old Trafford on September 17th 1981, which was won by Lancashire.

— NO ROTATION —

Between December 6th 1975 and February 28th 1976, United kept an unchanged team in 13 consecutive League and five FA Cup ties:

Stepney
Forsyth
Houston
Daly, B
Greenhoff
Buchan
Coppell
McIlroy
Pearson
Macari
Hill

The substitutes, however, changed several times.

— SHORT BUT SWEET —

Players whose United careers were over soon after they began:

- The shortest United playing career will almost certainly remain with one man – goalkeeper Nick Culkin who played a grand total of 18 seconds for the club. During a match against Arsenal at Highbury in 1999, Culkin replaced Raimond van der Gouw in the second minute of added time after an unfortunate meeting between the Dutchman's cheekbone and Martin Keown. United were leading 2–1 thanks to two Roy Keane goals and Arsenal were applying serious pressure when Culkin took to the field. He got 18 seconds of play and one touch on the ball. As the ref blew the final whistle the ball was in the air after his goalkick. Culkin can thus claim a clean sheet, but moved to Bristol Rovers soon after.
- Peter Beardsley played only 45 minutes of football for United in a League Cup tie against Bournemouth before going on to enjoy a notable career elsewhere.
- United player Tommy Bogan had one of the shortest international careers on record, as he was injured after only two minutes of his Scotland debut against England at Hampden in April 1945 and had to leave the field. He was never picked again.
- Mark Dempsey came on as substitute against Spartak Varna at Old Trafford in November 1983 for his United debut, but did not make his league debut until December 1985. This was also his only first team league appearance. Dempsey is now involved with coaching United's youngsters at Carrington.
- Joe Astley made only two appearances for Newton Heath, in March 1926 and April 1927. In the latter he received a knee injury after only 12 minutes and never played again for the club

— MR MANCHESTER UNITED —

In 2002, Martin Zdravkov, a Bulgarian, changed his name to 'Manchester United'.

— OVER EXPOSURE —

Over a 72-hour period in May 1988 – 7th, 8th, 9th – United played three games at Old Trafford: Wimbledon and Portsmouth in the league and Manchester City in Arthur Albiston's testimonial match. Despite United finishing second in the league to Liverpool – albeit by a distance of nine points – the Wimbledon game attracted a crowd of just 28,040.

— FA CUP FINAL GOALSCORERS —

Mark Hughes, Eric Cantona and Bryan Robson have all scored for United three times in FA Cup finals. United's other FA Cup final goalscorers are:

David Herd (2)
Jack Rowley (2)
Norman Whiteside (2)
Ruud van Nistelrooy (2)
Sandy Turnbull
John Anderson
Stan Pearson
Denis Law
Jimmy Greenhoff
Stuart Pearson
Ray Wilkins
Frank Stapleton
Sammy McIlroy
Gordon McQueen
Arnold Muhren
Lee Martin
Brian McClair
Tommy Taylor
Teddy Sheringham
Paul Scholes
Cristiano Ronaldo

— LONG SERVICE —

Jack Rowley has the longest United career, spanning 17 years and 98 days between his first appearance on October 23rd 1937 and his last on January 29th 1955.

Steve Coppell holds the record of the most consecutive games for United, 206 between January 13th 1977 and November 7th 1981.

Allenby Chilton was an ever present in the United league side for three consecutive seasons – 1951/52, 1952/53 and 1953/54. This record is only bettered by Steve Coppell – four in a row between 1977/78 and 1980/81.

— THEY SAID IT —

"It's one of the things I wish to God I'd had the opportunity of doing – being manager of Manchester United."
Noel Cantwell

"Came as a boy and left as an old man."
Tony Dunne on Wilf McGuinness

"Who is your favourite manager?"
"The manager of Stringfellows."
George Best answers a reporter's question

"Good day for hanging."
Frank O'Farrell as he arrived at Old Trafford on the day he was dismissed

"He came as a stranger and left as a stranger."
Denis Law on former United manager Frank O'Farrell

"Come on, my bonny boys."
Dave Sexton's last words to his team as they took the field before he was sacked

"It's the ultimate pressure job, but you know that and I'm delighted I accepted although I got the sack in the end."
Dave Sexton

"You can have my home number, but please remember not to call during *The Sweeney*."
Ron Atkinson gets friendly with journalists on the United beat after being appointed boss

"No, I am not a Catholic – but I'm willing to be converted."
Ron Atkinson, the first non-Roman Catholic United manager in 30 years

"One man stopped me winning the championship for Manchester United. Not once, but three times. His name? Ian Rush."
Ron Atkinson

"Big Ron From Old Swan Signs On."
Flag on Liverpool's Kop after Atkinson was sacked

"United's list of signings from our City Ground reads like a Who's Who. Perhaps United haven't signed the one who could have sorted them out once and for all. I'm referring to Old Big Head here. I'm long in the tooth. I've got a middle-aged spread and, quite frankly, one way or another I've shot it now. But if someone at Old Trafford had the courage, conviction or whatever it needed over the years to say: 'Let's go Cloughie', who knows what might have happened?"
Brian Clough

— FESTIVE FOOTBALL —

Top-flight football on Christmas Day was a regular feature until the 1950s. United's last game on Christmas Day was against Luton Town in 1957, when a crowd of 39,444 saw a 3–0 United win. The Reds played the same Luton side a day later at Kenilworth Road, drawing 2–2.

— NAUGHTY LADS —

Harry Gregg and Noel Cantwell were both sent off for United reserves against Burnley in a Central League match in February 1965.

— A FRANK EXCHANGE OF VIEWS —

After leading 2–0, United had shipped three goals away to Nottingham Forest in December 1984. The tension had been building for weeks, with goalkeeper Gary Bailey unsettled in Manchester and angry at his team-mates. Bailey walked in the dressing-room and said: "I am sick and tired of our defence giving away silly goals."

In the bestselling book *We're the Famous Man United* he continues: "I had a go at Gordon McQueen and told him that he was all over the place defensively. He told me that I wasn't good enough, adding that he thought I was a coward. I wasn't a coward. I put myself all over the place and had the bumps to show for it. So I walked across to confront Gordon. In classic university style I wanted to debate the issue. In classic working-class style he punched me hard in the face. One person held me back and twelve held him back. Thank goodness they did because he would have killed me."

— BRAINY REDS —

The following United players were all university graduates:

Gary Bailey (Witts in South Africa)
Warren Bradley (Durham)
Albert Broome (Victoria)
Steve Coppell (Liverpool)
Alan Gowling (Manchester)
Kevin Moran (Dublin)
Mike Pinner (Cambridge)

— SECOND HALF SURGE —

Newton Heath led Walsall Town Swifts 1–0 at half time in April 1895 and went on to win 9–0. Eight goals in one half remains a United record.

— MOVING HOMES —

The last league game played at Bank Street, one of United's former grounds in Clayton, was against Tottenham Hotspur on January 22nd 1910. United won 5–0 in front of 7,000 fans with goals from Roberts (2), Connor, Hooper and Meredith.

United's next game was at the club's new Old Trafford home, resplendent with an 80,000 capacity which earned the club the 'Moneybags United' tag. The stadium's grand opening went well as United led 3–1 after 74 minutes against Liverpool. Then it was spoiled as the visitors scored three times to record a 4–3 victory.

— THE ANGLO-ITALIAN CUP —

United played in this competition in season 1972/73. Placed in Group One, they played two games at home and two away, but despite being undefeated failed to qualify for the semi-finals:

Date	Opponents	Result	Scorers	Attendance
Feb 21st	Fiorentina (H)	Drew 1–1	Holton	23,951
Mar 21st	Lazio (A)	Drew 0–0		52,834
Apr 1st	Bari (H)	Won 3–1	Law, Storey-Moore, Martin	14,302
May 2nd	Verona (A)	Won 4–1	Charlton 2, Olney, Fletcher	8,168

— FERGIE AND FRIENDS —

"Football eh, bloody hell!"

"You can't go into a club and tell people their fitness is terrible, that they're bevvying, they're playing too much golf, and their ground is filthy. You simply have to improve things bit by bit."

"You can have the best collection of footballers ever, but if there is no-one driving the bus, you'll not get there."

"He's so greedy for success that if his grandkids beat him at cards he sends them to bed without any supper."
Gary Pallister on Alex Ferguson

"After ten years I might know the manager quite well but I still don't know how he picks his teams."
Brian McClair on Alex Ferguson

"Football, eh? Bloody hell!"
Alex Ferguson after his finest hour, winning the treble in Barcelona

— MOVING MEMORIAL —

The Munich Memorial is in its fourth location. It was originally above the directors' entrance in the South Stand, but was moved to the outside wall of 'K' Stand following re-development. It then went onto the wall at the right side of the East Stand before moving to its current site on the left hand side wall of the same stand.

The first memorial was unveiled by manager Matt Busby on February 25th 1960 and had been designed by local architect M.J. Vipond and constructed by Messers Jaconello Ltd. of Manchester, at a cost of £2,100. It was a replica of Old Trafford from a bird's eye view. Green slabs of faience (glazed porcelain) marked out the pitch, incised with black and gold glass letters forming an inscription and the names of those who lost their lives.

The terraces, gangways and so on were all to scale with the stand roofs and perimeter path worked from solid quartzite, enclosed by red Balmoral granite which formed the boundary wall of the ground. Two teak figures representing a player and spectator stood either side of a laurel wreath and a ball, which was inscribed '1958'. It was flanked by two torch lights, symbolising the eternal flame of memory. The second and third version of the memorial are simpler copies which have lost many of the features of the original, which was badly damaged during building work in the 1970s and was walled up by the new development. Only the teak figure group was saved from the original.

— CAP THAT —

Jackie Blanchflower is the only outfield player ever to wear a cap in an FA Cup final. United's emergency 'keeper took over in goal from the injured Ray Wood in the 1957 final and wore a cap to keep the sun out of his eyes. United lost the game 2–1 to Aston Villa.

— FA CUP TRIVIA —

- A 7–1 defeat by Burnley in the 1901 competition is United's heaviest cup defeat to date.
- Stan Crowther played for both Aston Villa and United in the 1958 competition. He also played for Villa against United in the 1957 final.
- Lee Martin was the first left-back to score in a final, when he netted the only goal of the 1990 replay against Crystal Palace.
- Sheffield United were drawn against United four times in five years – 1990, 1993, 1994, 1995 – with all the matches being played at Bramall Lane. United won a tight FA Cup 6th round game 1–0 against the Blades in 1990, the South Yorkshire team gaining revenge in the 1992/93 season with a 2–1 win. A season later a single Mark Hughes goal was enough to send United through a third round tie. Amazingly, the Blades again drew United at home in the third round the following season, 1994/95, with goals from Hughes and Cantona again seeing United through.
- Incredibly, United had a similar run against Chelsea in the same decade. In 1994 the two teams met in the final at Wembley, United winning 4–0. Two years later the Reds beat the Blues 2–1 in a Villa Park semi-final, David Beckham scoring the winner. Becks was again on target in United's dramatic 5–3 third round victory at Stamford Bridge, and the following season the Reds won a quarter-final replay 2–0 in London to make it four cup wins in five years over Chelsea.
- Bill Foulkes played in 61 consecutive FA Cup ties for United over a 13 year period.
- The 17,987 who watched the 1995 semi-final replay against Crystal Palace at Villa Park was the smallest at this stage of the competition for 93 years.
- In March 1963, United won their third, fourth, fifth and sixth round ties in the space of 27 days, due to severe weather disrupting the fixture list. United went on to win the cup, defeating Leicester City 3–1 at Wembley.
- Martin Buchan is the only man to have captained a team to cup success on both sides of the border, winning the Scottish Cup with Aberdeen in 1970 and the FA Cup with United in 1977.
- United played Watford at Highbury in the first ever FA Cup third place play-off in 1970, winning 2–0 thanks to two Brian Kidd goals. The idea to stage the game was a largely commercial decision. The FA wanted a money-spinning diversion for their members who were in the capital for the final. Previously, this

had been provided by a tie between an old England and a young England side, but interest had waned and the play-off idea was hatched at Lancaster Gate. It was a mistake. Instead of being a lucrative and consolatory exercise, it became an unpopular poor man's cup final which never caught the public's imagination. Highbury was a quarter full, partly because at 50 shillings (£2.50p) for a seat, they were more expensive than they had been for the semi-finals, and the fare down South added to the cost. Despite the lack of enthusiasm, the FA persisted with the third place play-off. However, just 5,031 watched Stoke City beat Everton at Selhurst Park the following year. Common sense eventually prevailed in 1974 and the game was disbanded. For United, the victory in 1970 remains one of the least regarded honours in the Old Trafford trophy cabinet.

— DOUBLE DUTIES —

In season 1993/94, Dennis Irwin and Steve Bruce each played in 62 first class games for United, one of those as substitute. Their endeavours were worth it as United won the Premiership and FA Cup.

— BUNG BAN —

United were banned by the FA from playing friendlies, either at home or away, in 1969 after being found guilty of making illegal payments.

— COLOUR BLIND —

The infamous match against Southampton at the Dell on April 13th 1996, when United, losing 3–0 at half time, changed their grey shirts for blue and white, was not the first time that the club had done this. On Febuary 21st 1903, while playing Everton in an FA Cup second round tie, United changed from their red shirts to blue and white at half time, due to atrocious weather conditions. They also lost this game, but only 1–0.

— FOUNDING FATHERS —

Manchester United were founder members of the Central League, the old name for the reserve team's league competition, in 1911/12.

— NIGHTMARE SEASON —

In 1930/31, United set a club record by conceding 115 goals, losing 27 games and winning only seven times. Not surprisingly, the club finished well adrift at the bottom of the First Division. The final game of the season, a 4–4 draw against Middlesbrough at Old Trafford, was watched by just 3,969. The mood among Reds did not lift over the summer of 1931, and the gate of 3,507 for the first home game of the season against Aston Villa remains the lowest for a United game. That one ended in defeat, too . . .

— JUST HIS LUCK —

Beaumont Asquith made his United debut at Charlton on September 2nd 1939, the day before the Second World War was declared. This was his only United appearance. United lost the game 2–0 in front of just 8,608 – the same fixture the previous season attracted 23,721. United lost that game too – 7–1.

— TWO FOR ONE —

On May 7th 1921, a crowd of 10,000 watched United play Derby County in a First Division fixture. After this game, already relegated Stockport County played Leicester Fosse in a Second Division fixture, as Edgeley Park had been closed by the FA because of crowd trouble. Only 13 people paid to watch this game (officially the lowest attendance for a football league fixture), although many remained from the United fixture to watch for free. The only other league ground to have staged two games on the same day is Hartlepool's Victoria Park.

— TED THE RED —

Ted MacDougall, who was signed in September 1972 by Frank O'Farrell for £200,000 – a record at the time for a Third Division player – had scored a record nine goals for Bournemouth in their 11–0 FA Cup first round win against Margate the previous year. Unfortunately, MacDougall couldn't reproduce the same form for United. The bustling forward scored just five goals in 18 appearances and was transfer-listed when Tommy Docherty took over in February 1973. He soon moved to West Ham, and went on to play for nine clubs in total. By the end of his career he had became the first Scottish player since Denis Law to score more than 200 league goals.

— CROWDS —

- Only once since 1946/47 have Manchester City had a better seasonal average attendance than United and that was in 1954/55, when City averaged a massive 34,946, compared to United's 34,077.
- United's single 1999 European Super Cup defeat by Lazio in Monaco was watched by only 14,461 spectators. The game was played in Monte Carlo at the home of Monaco, which has a capacity of just 16,000.
- Wembley cup final attendances over the years were generally given at 100,000.

However, the official attendances for United's finals up until 1985 were:

1948: 99,842
1957: 99,225
1958: 99,756
1963: 99,604
1976: 99,115
1977: 99,252
1979: 99,219
1983: 99,059 Replay: 91,534
1985: 99,445

(Wembley became an all-seated stadium with an 80,000 capacity after the Hillsborough disaster).

— SUPER SCOTS —

Martin Buchan, Gordon Strachan and Brian McClair have all won the Scottish Footballer of the Year Award – in 1971, 1980 and 1987 respectively.

— HERDING INSTINCT —

On November 26th 1966, David Herd scored against three different Sunderland goalkeepers in the same match. Regular keeper Jim Montgomery went off injured and was replaced by John Parke and then Charlie Hurley. Herd scored four in United's 5–0 victory.

Incidentally, in May 1951, Herd played in the same Stockport County team as his father Alec, who had played alongside Matt Busby for City.

— ENGLAND CAPTAINS —

David Beckham is the most recent United player to captain England

The following players with links to United have all captained England:

David Beckham, Bryan Robson, Ray Wilkins, David Platt, Paul Ince, Bobby Charlton, Gary Neville and Peter Beardsley.

— AVOIDING THE CUMBRIANS —

United have never played Carlisle United in the league. When Carlisle were promoted to the top flight in 1974, it corresponded with United's relegation. The two clubs did meet in the FA Cup in 1977/78, drawing 1–1 at Brunton Park in front of a crowd of 21,710. United won the replay 4–2 in front of 54,156 fans.

— PLACE NAME —

Players with the same name as an area of Manchester:

(Gordon) Clayton
(Thomas) Chorlton
(Aaron) Hulme

There was also a reserve team player called Beswick.

— BATTING AND BOWLING REDS —

The following United players also played cricket:

Andy Goram: 43 times for Scotland
Arnie Sidebottom: Yorkshire and England
Freddie Goodwin: Lancashire
Noel Cantwell: Ireland
David Herd: Minor county level
David Sadler: Kent schoolboy level
Phil Neville: Lancashire schoolboy level
Bill Dennis: Minor county level and professional with Milnrow

In addition, the father of former England skipper Michael Atherton was once on United's books.

— HIGH FIVES —

United's highest competitive draw was 5–5 against Lincoln City on October 16th 1895. On a post-season tour of the United States in 1950, United drew 6–6 with Atlas of Mexico.

— PENALTY PAIN —

United have been knocked out of Europe twice in penalty shoot-outs. In March 1985, the Reds lost 5–4 to Videoton of Hungary in the UEFA Cup quarter-finals, having drawn 1–1 on aggregate. In September 1992, United were beaten 4–3 on spot-kicks by Torpedo Moscow, again in the UEFA Cup, after both games ended 0–0. The game, United's 100th in European competition, also marked Gary Neville's debut after he came on as a substitute.

— THE McSHANES —

Harry McShane, who played 57 times for United between 1950 and 1954, was the PA announcer at Old Trafford in the late 1960s and early 1970s. He was also the founder of the Manchester United Old Players' Association. His actor son Ian is famous for his role as the antiques dealer in *Lovejoy*, but also latterly as Al Swearingen in US western series *Deadwood*.

— PLAY-OFF DEFEAT —

In 1895, Newton Heath's third placed finish in the Second Division earned them the right to play Stoke City, who had finished third from bottom of the First Division, in a one-off play-off match to determine which club would play top flight football the following season. Stoke won the game 3–0 in the Potteries. The same team had knocked the Heathens out of the FA Cup that season in the first round.

— EUROPEAN PLAYER OF THE YEAR —

The following United players have all won the continent's top individual award:

Denis Law (1964)
Bobby Charlton (1966)
George Best (1968)

— MINOR COMPETITIONS —

In 1985/86, United played Everton twice in the Screen Sport Super Cup. This competition was arranged for English clubs who were banned from Europe following Heysel. Everton won both games, 4–2 at Old Trafford and 1–0 at Goodison.

In 1988, to celebrate the 100th anniversary of the Football League, United were entered into the Mercantile Credit Trophy after they had finished in the top eight of Division One. Everton were beaten 1–0 in the first game at Old Trafford in front of just 16,439 fans. Newcastle visited Manchester for the 'semi-final' and were beaten 2–0 after extra time in front of an even lower crowd of 14,968. That set up a final tie against Arsenal at Villa Park. The Gunners won 2–1 watched by 20,000 fans.

— STARTING OUT IN THE LEAGUE CUP —

United drew their first ever Football League Cup tie 1–1 against Exeter City at St James Park on October 19th 1960, watched by a 14,500 crowd. They won the Old Trafford replay 4–1. United progressed to a second round tie away to Bradford Park Avenue, where they were defeated 2–1 in front of 4,670 – the lowest crowd to watch a competitive post-war United game.

United chose not to enter the League Cup again until 1967, when they fielded a weakened side against Blackpool in their first League Cup game for seven years – and lost 5–1.

— SEVEN UP —

On December 31st 1892 Newton Heath defeated Derby County 7–1. Seven days later, on January 7th 1893, they lost 7–1 against Stoke City. It is worth noting, however, that in the latter game, United only had 10 men, with centre half Stewart having to play in goal, after regular custodian Warner missed the train.

When United set their record 7–0 league victory over Aston Villa at Old Trafford on March 8th 1950, Charlie Mitten scored a hat-trick of penalties. Prior to taking his third, the Villa goalkeeper asked him where he was going to put it. "Same place as the other two," came the reply, which he proceeded to do.

— VERY EARLY BATH —

Liam O'Brien was sent off for United against Southampton at the Dell on January 3rd 1987, after only 85 seconds – the fastest dismissal in the Reds' history.

"I still don't think I deserved it," he said years later. "It was the first tackle of the game and I was not the sort of player that went out to 'do' any other professional. I was devastated as it was the first live game shown in Ireland. All my family and friends were watching it – so I was understandably gutted."

Despite losing O'Brien so soon after the kick-off, 10-man United still managed to earn a point from a 1–1 draw.

— YOU'VE ONLY COME TO SEE UNITED! —

Top 10 attendances at Manchester United away league fixtures:

Date	Result	Venue	Attendance
September 4th 1957	Everton 3 United 3	Goodison Park	72,077
September 20th 1947	Manchester City 0 United 0	Maine Road	71,364
September 22nd 1951	Tottenham 2 United 0	White Hart Lane	70,882
December 28th 1957	Manchester City 2 United 2	Maine Road	70,483
August 22nd 1962	Everton 3 United 1	Goodison Park	69,501
September 6th 1930	Chelsea 6 United 2	Stamford Bridge	68,648
February 19th 1949	Aston Villa 2 United 1	Villa Park	68,354
February 28th 1959	Arsenal 3 United 2	Highbury	67,162
September 2nd 1959	Chelsea 3 United 6	Stamford Bridge	66,579
October 14th 1950	Arsenal 3 United 0	Highbury	66,150

— THE ARSE —

Memorable encounters with the Reds from north London:

- On the final day of the 1951/52 season, Arsenal travelled to Old Trafford needing to defeat United by seven goals in order to pip the Reds to the First Division championship. The 53,651 crowd did indeed see seven goals, but the scoreline read United 6 Arsenal 1.
- Following a free-for-all punch-up between United and Arsenal players at Old Trafford on October 20th 1990, United were deducted one point and Arsenal two. It was the first time in history that teams had suffered such punishment but Arsenal still won the title.
- Both Dave Sexton (United manager) and Stewart Houston (United player) have been assistant managers at Arsenal.

— SCOTTISH LINKS —

- John McCartney, who captained Newton Heath in 1894, later became manager of Hearts. He was replaced at Tynecastle by his son Willie, who went on to manage Hibernian. After his death, United played a benefit match for his widow.
- Alex Ferguson was replaced as manager of East Stirlingshire by former United centre half Ian Ure. Ure played for the Dundee team which reached the semi-final of the European Cup in the 1960s – it remains one of Ferguson's favourite teams.
- Ten names associated with both United and Celtic: Jimmy Delaney, Roy Keane, Paddy Crerand, Lee Martin, Tommy Docherty, Lou Macari, Brian McClair, Tommy Bogan, Joe Cassidy and Gordon Strachan.
- Ten United players/staff who have been associated with Glasgow Rangers – Jimmy Nicholl, Andy Goram, Lee Martin, Phil Bardsley, Andrei Kanchelskis, Sir Alex Ferguson, Ray Wilkins, Alex Forsyth, John McCartney and Archie Montgomery.

— NOTHING LIKE THE FIRST TIME —

Some notable United debuts:

- Arthur Rowley, Jack's brother, made his United debut as an amateur guest player (from Wolves) against Liverpool on November 29th 1941 at the age of 15 years and 222 days, becoming United's youngest debutant at competitive level. However, he never played for the club in peacetime football.
- Arthur Albiston made his United FA Cup debut in the 1977 final. Other United FA Cup final debutants were Les Sealey (1990 replay) and Alan Davies (1983). Sealey is also the only on-loan player ever to play in a FA Cup final.
- Ten players who scored on their United debuts: Gordon Strachan, Lou Macari, Wyn Davies, Ian Storey-Moore, Paul Scholes, Danny Wallace, Neil Webb, Denis Law, Alex Dawson and Bobby Charlton.
- Shay Brennan made his United debut as an outside-left, against Sheffield Wednesday in the first game after Munich, but won two league championship medals and a European Cup winners' medal as a full-back.

— 'TOTTMAN' —

United's players had barely finished celebrating the 1983 FA Cup win before they flew to Swaziland for a post season tour. The tiny landlocked country in southern Africa was chosen because political sanctions prevented United playing in neighbouring South Africa.

United played Tottenham Hotspur twice in the Lobamba national stadium, winning one and losing one. In between, United and Spurs combined to form a single team: 'Tottman'. This bizarre hybrid beat a Swaziland XI 6–1.

— SELECTED FIRSTS —

- United's first ever Football League game was against Blackburn Rovers on September 3rd 1892 at Ewood Park in front of 8,000 spectators. United lost 4–3.
- United's first ever Premiership game was at Sheffield United's Bramall Lane on August 15th 1992, when the home side won 2–1. Brian Deane scored the Premiership's first ever goal in the match.
- The first two league meetings between United and Liverpool in season 1895/96 saw a total of 15 goals scored, Liverpool winning 7–1 at Anfield and Newton Heath winning 5–2 at Bank Street.

— TAKING ON THE VILLANS —

Reversals of fortune against the Villa:

- On August 30th 1930, United were leading Aston Villa 3–0, but went on to lose 4–3.
- In January 2002, Villa were leading United 2–0 in an FA Cup third round tie, with only 13 minutes remaining, but three goals in five minutes from Ruud Van Nistelrooy and Ole Gunnar Solskjaer saw United win 3–2.

— CAPE CRUSADER —

Jackie Cape scored perhaps the most important goal in United's history, the second in the 2–0 win at Millwall on the last day of season 1933/34, in a match that United had to win to remain in the Second Division.

— GOALSCORING FEATS —

- On November 3rd 1962, United defeated Ipswich Town 5–3 at Portman Road, with Denis Law scoring four. On September 7th 1963, United returned to Portman Road and won 7–2, Law this time scoring three.
- Against Chelsea at Old Trafford on November 3rd 1973, United were losing 2–0 with only 90 seconds remaining. Goals from George Graham and Tony Young gave United a 2–2 draw.
- Andy Cole created a Premiership record when he scored five of United's goals in the 9–0 victory over Ipswich at Old Trafford on March 4th 1995.

— THE MANCHESTER DERBY —

- In the Maine Road derby match of March 13th 1974, Lou Macari and Mike Doyle were both sent off for fighting, but refused to leave the pitch, so referee Clive Thomas took both teams off until things calmed down.
- The 100th meeting between City and United took place at Old Trafford on 22nd March 1980. United won 1–0.

— FA CUP ODDITIES —

- Johnny Anderson scored only two goals for United in his 40-game career and one of those was United's fourth in the 1948 FA Cup final against Blackpool.
- In 1965 and 1970, United were drawn against Leeds in the FA Cup semi-finals and it required two games and three games respectively to decide the winner, with Leeds winning 1–0 on each occasion and United failing to score in any of the five games.
- United have lost only one FA Cup tie out of eight against Liverpool since the war. This includes two semi-finals and two finals.
- In 1971/72 Stoke City knocked United out of both the FA Cup and Football League Cup.
- United have only met Newcastle United three times in the FA Cup – 1909, 1990 and 1999 – and have gone on to win the cup in each of those seasons.

— 'MAGNIFICO' —

There's only one Ronaldo!

Top continental Reds:

Eric Cantona: Better than Best? Some might say. Non?
Cristiano Ronaldo: Put the mad in Madeira. World class.
Ruud van Nistelrooy: A goal a game kept the long face happy.
Peter Schmeichel: Well, what did you expect from someone born in Gladsaxe?
Jaap Stam: A rock at the heart of the United defence until his book annoyed Fergie.
Ole Gunnar Solskjaer: From the fjords with baby-faced love. Used to support Liverpool.
Dwight Yorke: Goals and girls. He scored both.

Andrei Kanchelskis: Faster than a Ukrainian election count (pre 2004).
Mikael Silvestre: Oh Mikey you're so fine. Even with your bubble head.
Arnold Muhren: United director Maurice Watkins lists the Dutchman as his favourite ever Red.
Nemanja Vidic: The Serb hardman is already a Red legend.
Ronny Johnsen: Fewer than 100 Reds league games in six years due to injury, but the Norwegian was a key part of the treble-winning side.
Patrice Evra: Dodgy start, superb second season for the French defender.

— FASCINATING FACTS —

- The first time Newton Heath played Luton Town in the league, in September 1897, the latter won 2–1 away. Of the 18 subsequent visits by the Hatters, United have won them all, scoring 57 goals and conceding just eight in the process.
- Leyton Orient travelled to Manchester to play United on February 7th 1925 and before the game, the transfer of Albert Pape, an Orient player, was agreed between the two clubs. United won the game 4–2 – with Pape one of the scorers.
- Barnsley have only ever defeated United four times in the league, despite the teams having met 32 times.
- United failed to win at Bolton for 13 consecutive seasons, between 1950/51 and 1962/63. Until recently, Bolton were the only club to have won more games than they had lost against United.
- When United defeated Huddersfield Town 6–0 at Old Trafford on November 5th 1949, the Town 'keeper saved two penalties, both taken by Charlie Mitten.
- United have only faced Aldershot once at competitive level and that was in a League Cup second round tie on September 9th 1970, the Reds winning 3–1 with goals from George Best, Brian Kidd and Denis Law in front of 18,509 fans.
- In season 1983/84, Forest won 2–1 at Old Trafford and 2–0 at the City Ground. All of their goals were scored by players who had at some point played for United – Viv Anderson (2), Gary Birtles and Peter Davenport.
- When United defeated Southampton 2–0 at the Dell on March 24th 1990, Colin Gibson scored with his last kick before being substituted by Neil Webb. The second goal was scored by Mark Robbins who scored with his first kick after coming on as substitute for Mark Hughes.

- Bury were drawn at home against United in the fourth round of the 1987/88 League Cup, but asked for the game to be switched to Old Trafford, where they lost 2–1. They were drawn together again in 1998/99 and lost 2–0 after extra time. One of the United goals was scored by Eric Nevland, which was the Norwegian striker's only goal for the club.
- United's 8–1 victory against Nottingham Forest at the City Ground on February 6th 1998 was the biggest away win in the club's history.
- Middlesbrough's 3–2 win at Old Trafford on December 19th 1998 was the first time they had won there since 1929/30, a period that took in some 22 games. United won 17 games and the remainder were draws.
- Sir Alex Ferguson's 600th match in charge of United was against Newcastle at Old Trafford in January 2001, with United winning 3–1. Paul Scholes scored twice in what was his 300th United game. His first goal was his 50th for the club.
- United clinched their place back in the First Division with a 2–2 draw at Notts County on April 19th 1975.

— SCORED TOO SOON —

West Brom scored against United after only 12 seconds at Old Trafford on December 15th 1951. They eventually lost 5–1.

— TALL REDS —

Peter Fletcher	1972–73	6ft 5in
Peter Schmeichel	1991–99	6ft 4in
Gary Pallister	1989–1998	6ft 4in
Gordon McQueen	1978–1985	6ft 4in
Gary Walsh	1986–1995	6ft 3in
Gary Bailey	1978–1986	6ft 2in
Paul McGrath	1982–1999	6ft 2in
Fred Goodwin	1954–1960	6ft 2in
Mark Bosnich	1989–1991 & 1999–2001	6ft 2in
Ray Van Der Gouw	1996–2001	6ft 2in
Steve Patterson	1976–1980	6ft 2in

* Despite the terrace song which actually exaggerated his height, 'big' Jim Holton was actually a mere 6ft 1in.

— PEOPLE POWER —

- Gary Birtles failed to score in his first 25 League games for United after having enjoyed a prolific scoring record at Nottingham Forest.
- Roger Byrne, while on his way to training one morning, crashed his car into Matt Busby's garden wall.
- Johnny Carey once played a complete 90 minutes in goal for United, against Sunderland away on February 18th 1953. The game ended in a 2–2 draw.
- Laurie Cassidy made only four appearances for United in his nine years at the club. He later joined Oldham before retiring in 1957. He had always been a part-time player combining his football with teaching and was later headmaster of St Patrick's School in Collyhurst, recommending Brian Kidd to United. The school had earlier produced both Wilf McGuinness and Nobby Stiles.
- Ian Donald, a United player in the late 1960s and early 1970s was later to become chairman of Aberdeen.
- John Connelly, who made a name for himself as a winger with Burnley, United and Blackburn, later ran a fish and chip shop in his native Burnley.
- Mark Higgins retired from playing at the end of season 1983/84, due to a pelvic injury, but returned to league football with Bury in 1987.
- Gordon Hill was once slapped across the head by his ever stern captain Martin Buchan for not coming back to help out in defence. Hill, who was nicknamed 'Merlin' for his wing wizardry, was also substituted in both the 1976 and 1977 FA Cup Finals.
- Although born in Aberdeen, Alex Dawson represented England Schoolboys, as his family had moved south.
- Dion Dublin was given a free transfer by Norwich City in 1988, but was to cost United £1m when signed from Cambridge in August 1992.

— CAPTAIN MARVEL —

Former United wing-half Eddie McIlvenny captained the United States to a memorable 1–0 World Cup victory over England in 1950.

— HAT-TRICK HEROES —

- In season 1925/26 Chris Taylor scored six goals for United – remarkably, made up of two hat-tricks.
- Five United players have scored hat-tricks for England: Jack Rowley, Tommy Taylor, Bobby Charlton, Bryan Robson and Paul Scholes. Taylor grabbed two hat-tricks, while Charlton managed four.
- Andrei Kanchelskis scored a hat-trick against Manchester City in November 1994, the first in a derby game for 24 years.
- Alex Dawson scored a hat-trick in three successive reserve team games during season 1959/60. He was also the youngest United player to score a hat-trick when he scored three against Fulham in the 1958 FA Cup semi-final replay at Highbury, aged 18 years and 35 days.
- Andy Ritchie was also 18 when he scored three against Leeds in March 1979. Ritchie was dropped for the next game.
- Sammy McIlroy scored a hat-trick in United's 5–0 win over Wolves in October 1981. He kept his place for the following game, before being dropped to make way for new £1.5m record signing Bryan Robson.
- The oldest United player to score a hat-trick is Teddy Sheringham against Southampton on October 28th 2000 – 34 years and 208 days
- Henry Boyd scored a hat-trick in the first two Newton Heath fixtures of season1897/98, a 5–0 win over Lincoln City at home and a 4–0 win over Burton Swifts away. His shooting boots deserted him after that as he didn't score again until December.
- In November 1938, Tottenham's Willie Hall scored a hat-trick for England at Old Trafford against Ireland in less than three minutes.

— THE LEAGUE'S CENTENARY —

The Football League's centenary celebrations in 1987 were highly ambitious. The first event, a game between a Football League XI and 'the Rest of the World' at Wembley featured three United players: Bryan Robson, Norman Whiteside and Paul McGrath.

Robbo and Norm scored the goals in the 3–0 victory for the League watched by over 60,000 fans. Maradona's appearance created a furore when it became known that, although only half-fit, he had demanded a £100,000 fee, which the League, who had sold the television rights to a huge global audience, paid.

— INTERNATIONAL REDS —

Charlie Roberts was United's first England international, when he was selected during the 1904/05 season. Despite being an outstanding defender who was good enough to lead United to two league championships and their first FA Cup, Roberts was only capped three times for England. Many thought that was because Roberts was a founder member of the Players' Union and his involvement in the organisation found little favour with the game's authorities.

Other notable Red international feats include:

- Jackie Blanchflower appeared in 12 Northern Ireland internationals alongside brother Danny, captain of Tottenham's 1961 'Double' side.
- The England back three against Northern Ireland in October 1954 was entirely made up of United players – goalkeeper Ray Wood and full backs Bill Foulkes and Roger Byrne.
- Mike Pinner made only four appearances for United, but won 51 caps for the England amateur side.
- Gary Neville won his first full England cap against Japan in June 1995 after only 19 United league games.
- Viv Anderson was the first black player to play for England. Laurie Cunningham was the second.
- Shay Brennan, from Wythenshawe in Manchester, was named in the original 40 players for England's 1962 World Cup squad. He was not selected for the final 22 and went on to be capped by the Republic of Ireland. He was the first player to be capped by the Republic and not born there.
- Former United striker Peter Davenport's England career lasted only 17 minutes, as a substitute against Republic of Ireland in March 1985.
- Six Newton Heath players were regulars in the Welsh side during season 1889/90.
- Steve Bruce, although capped by England at youth team level, never managed a full cap, although Jackie Charlton tried to persuade him to play for the Republic of Ireland in 1993.

— LIFESAVER —

Fred Kennedy, a United player in the 1920s, was presented with a medal by the Humane Society after saving a woman from drowning.

THE MAN UTD MISCELLANY

— EURO WINNERS —

United players who have won the UEFA European Championship:

Holland 1988: Arnold Muhren (1982–85)
Denmark 1992: Peter Schmeichel (1991–99)
France 2000: Fabien Barthez (2000–03) and Laurent Blanc (2001–03)

— AGEING WELL —

In 1949, Neil McBain was coach of United's future World Club Championship opponents Estudiantes. Two years earlier he had come out of retirement, while New Brighton's secretary manager, to play in goal in a Third Division North fixture against Hartlepool at the age of 51 years and four months, making him the oldest player ever to play in the football league – a record which still stands today. As a matter of interest, he had made his debut for Ayr United fully 32 years earlier.

— TRIO OF ROBERTSONS —

United signed three unrelated players all with the surname Robertson (Alex, Alex and Tom) in the space of five days in May 1903.

— RUGBY REDS —

Former United goalkeeper John Sutcliffe represented England at rugby union against New Zealand in 1899 before joining Bolton Wanderers, as a centre forward, to pursue a footballing career, winning five England caps. By the time he joined United, he had moved back to play between the posts.

Sutcliffe, United's goalkeeper in the 1903/04 season, was the last person to play at international level for England at both football and rugby union.

Other rugby Reds include Tommy O'Neil, United full back in the early 1970s, who was capped at schoolboy level at rugby union and 1970s United striker Stuart Pearson who played rugby union for Sale's reserves in 1985.

— IT'S FOOTBALL, NOT BOXING —

Kevin Lewis, a United reserve, was given a five-match ban in December 1971 for attacking a referee. He never played for United again.

— SHARP IN THE BOX —

On returning to England in 1984 after spells with Bologna, Spal FC, Lecce, Rimini and FC Trento, red-haired former United midfielder Carlo Sartori, who was born in Italy but came to England as a child, became a registered knife sharpener.

— FRANK'S DOUBLE —

When Frank Stapleton scored against Brighton and Hove Albion in the 1983 FA Cup final, he became the first player to score in the final with two different teams. He had previously scored in the 1979 final for Arsenal against United in the Gunners' dramatic 3–2 injury-time win.

— SUPER SUBS —

- Well before the days of official substitutes (see below), David Gaskell became the first replacement used by United, coming on for goalkeeper Ray Wood in the 1956 FA Charity Shield against City at Maine Road. When Wood was injured, a United official remembered seeing Gaskell (a junior player who was just 16 years-old at the time and had travelled to the game by local bus) going into the ground. A call was put out over the tannoy system and he played in borrowed boots.
- After the rules were changed to allow substitutes in competitive games (only in the event of injury), the first named United substitute in the league was Noel Cantwell against Sheffield Wednesday on August 21st 1965. The first used league substitute was John Fitzpatrick against Tottenham on October 16th 1965, who came on for Denis Law.
- Ron Davies made ten appearances for United, all as substitute.

— COSTLY COCKNEY —

Alex Stepney's £55,000 move from Chelsea to United in 1966 was a then record fee for a goalkeeper.

— TANGLED WEBB —

The £1m transfer of Neil Webb from Nottingham Forest to United was the first set by a tribunal.

— SKIP TO THE BANK —

Lou Macari's £200,000 move from Celtic to United was a record between a Scottish and an English club.

— DEAR DEFENDERS —

The transfers of Gordon McQueen from Leeds (£450,000), Gary Pallister from Middlesbrough (£2.3m), Jaap Stam from PSV Eindhoven (£10.75m) and Rio Ferdinand from Leeds (£29m) all set new transfer records for a defender.

— BUSY LAD —

Tricky 80s winger Peter Barnes played for 20 different clubs at various levels, including Real Betis of Spain. Barnes still keeps in touch with the family who he lived with during his year in southern Spain.

— SHARED BIRTHDAY —

Companies which were formed in 1878, the same year as United:

- Mohawk Industries: an American company which supplies residential and commercial flooring and other home products. It is one of the two largest carpet manufacturers in the world and exchanged on the New York Stock Exchange under the listed security MHK. Whatever some fans may think, Ron Atkinson's rug wasn't made by them.
- The F.W. Woolworth Company (often referred to as 'Woolworth's') started as one of the original American five-and-dime stores before becoming a huge retail corporation. The first Woolworth's store was founded in 1878 by Frank Winfield Woolworth. The nearest one to Old Trafford is in Stretford Arndale, next to Superdrug.
- Venchi: the Italian gourmet chocolate manufacturer founded by artisan chocolatier Silvano Venchi, started out in Turin. The company gained immediate popularity throughout Italy with Nougatine – small bars made of crushed and caramelised hazelnuts coated in dark chocolate. Many of the 250 products in Venchi's collection are still handmade and distributed on demand.

— RED RELATIVES —

Some players with family ties at United and links to other football clubs:

Dick Duckworth (1903–1914)   Father of Richard, an ex-United junior who made over 300 league appearances with seven different clubs.

Joe Spence (1919–1933)   His son, Joe junior, played over 100 times for York City in the 1950s.

Charlie Mitten (1946–50)   His son Charlie played for United's reserves and Exeter. Grandson Paul was a United junior in the 1990s and great nephew Jonathan was the first signing for breakaway club FC United of Manchester.

Don Gibson (1950–55)   The onetime United wing-half married Matt Busby's daughter, Sheena.

Matt Gillespie (1896–1900)   Brother of ex-Manchester City player Billy Gillespie.

Jack Rowley (1937–55)   Brother of ex-West Brom, Fulham, Leicester and Shrewsbury striker, Arthur Rowley.

Frank Haydock (1958–63)   Brother of ex-Manchester City player William Haydock.

David Herd (1961–68)   Son of former Manchester City forward, Alec Herd.

Nobby Stiles (1960–71)   Brother-in-law of ex-United (1957–63), Leeds and West Brom midfielder Johnny Giles and father of ex-Leeds and Doncaster midfielder John Stiles.

Denis Law (1962–73)   Father of United press officer, Di Law.

Mick Martin (1972–75)   Son of Republic of Ireland Con, who played centre half or goalkeeper for Aston Villa.

Lou Macari (1973–84)   Father of ex-Stoke City players Mike and Paul Macari.

Joe Jordan (1978–81)   Father of ex-Bristol City players Andy and Tom Jordan.

Gary Bailey (1978–1986)	Son of former Ipswich goalkeeper Roy.
Mark Higgins (1985–86)	Son of John, who played for Bolton against United in the 1958 FA Cup final.
Steve Bruce (1987–96)	Father of Ipswich midfielder, Alex Bruce.
Peter Schmeichel (1991–99)	Father of Manchester City goalkeeper, Kaspar Schmeichel.
Chris Casper (1993–98)	Son of former Burnley striker, Frank Casper.
Jordi Cruyff (1996–98)	Son of Ajax and Barcelona legend, Johan Cruyff.
Wilf McGuinness (1953–58 and manager 1970)	Father of current United U-18 manager and assistant youth academy director, Paul McGuinness.
Tommy Docherty (manager 1972–77)	Father of ex-Burnley and Manchester City player, Michael Docherty.
Sir Alex Ferguson (manager 1986–)	Father of ex-United midfielder Darren (1990–94) and football agent, Jason Ferguson.
Bojan Djordjic (1999–2005)	His father, Ranko, played for Red Star Belgrade.

In addition to these United-related family relationships within football, ex-Red Juan Sebastian Veron's father, Juan Ramon Veron, was not only a member of the Estudiantes side that beat United in the Intercontinental Club Cup in 1968, *La Bruja* (the Witch) also scored with a header. Juan Sebastian, nicknamed *La Brujita* (The Little Witch), was not the first member of his family to play for an English club. That honour belongs to his uncle, striker Pedro Verde, who was at Sheffield United between 1978 and 1981.

Other United players with sporting family links include Paul Ince, whose cousin Nigel Benn was a super-middleweight world champion boxer and, of the current team, Ryan Giggs, whose brother, Rhodri Giggs plays on the left wing for non-league FC United of Manchester. Then, of course, there is Rio Ferdinand, whose brother Anton plays for West Ham – the pair are also nephews of Les Ferdinand, the much-travelled former England international striker.

— YOU WERE BORN WHERE? —

Rangoon, Burma: Charlie Mitten. Mitten's father was a boxer in the British Army.

Barnsley: Busby Babes Tommy Taylor and Mark Jones, plus the Greenhoff brothers hailed from this gritty Yorkshire town. As did Billy Wrigglesworth, who scored 10 goals in 37 appearances between 1937 and 1947.

Liverpool: John Gidman, Steve Coppell, Ron Atkinson and Wayne Rooney are all Scousers by birth.

Cork: Roy Keane, Liam Miller, Denis Irwin and Noel Cantwell.

Aberdeen: Martin Buchan, Denis Law, Alex Dawson, John Fitzpatrick, Graeme Hogg, Ian Moir, and 1930s star George Mutch all came from the Granite City.

Newcastle: Steve Bruce, Peter Beardsley, goalkeeper Ray Wood, Joe Spence who made over 500 United appearances and Bryan Robson, are all of Geordie stock.

Peshawar, Pakistan: George 'Cocky' Hunter, United's half-back in the First World War, was born in this exotic location.

Hamilton, Canada: The birthplace of 70s/80s defender Jimmy Nicholl.

Motherwell (within ten miles of): Joe Jordan, Brian McClair, Jimmy Delaney, Arthur Graham, Jack Picken, Tom Reid, David Herd, Charlie Rennox, Jim Holton, Harry McShane and Francis Burns – and Sir Matt Busby.

Edinburgh: Arthur Albiston, Darren Fletcher, Lou Macari and Gordon Strachan.

Jindinchuv-Hradec. Well where did you expect Karel Poborsky to come from? Stoke?

— ORIGINAL FEATURE —

The only part of the original 1909 ground which still exists at Old Trafford today is the tunnel in the centre of the South Stand, which led from the old dressing-rooms onto the pitch.

— OLD TRAFFORD ON THE WORLD STAGE —

In 1966 Old Trafford staged the following World Cup games: Hungary v Poland, Bulgaria v Portugal and Bulgaria v Hungary. All three matches drew crowds of less than 30,000.

— 'EL MANCHESTER? PFFT!' —

11 teams who've beaten United in Europe:

1. The first team to win a European game at Old Trafford weren't Milan, Barça or Real, but **Fenerbahce** of Istanbul, 1–0 winners in October 1996.

2. **Sporting Lisbon** blitzed United 5–0 away in the 1963/1964 Cup Winners' Cup. Which meant the 4–1 home victory and Denis Law's hat-trick counted for little.

3. **Tottenham Hotspur** beat United 2–0 in the 1964 Cup Winners' Cup. United won the home leg 4–1.

4. **Barcelona** put four past United without reply in a key Champions League game in 1994. Never repeat the words 'Stoitchov and Romario' to Steve Bruce or Gary Pallister.

5. Israeli champions **Maccabi Haifa** beat a youthful United side 3–0 in 2002. The game was played in Nicosia, Cyprus, because of the security situation in Israel.

6. **Athletic Bilbao** beat United 5–3 in a snowy Basque country in 1957. It was United's first defeat in Europe, but they overturned the result – winning 3–0 in the second leg.

7. United's record victory remains the 10–0 home win against **Anderlecht** in the first European game to be staged at Old Trafford, yet the Belgians have beaten United twice at home in the two meetings since.

8. United lost three of the six Champions' League group games in the 1996/97 season, but still qualified behind **Juventus**, who had edged United 1–0 home and away . . .

9. . . . Something **Borussia Dortmund** managed to do in the semi-final of the 1997 competition.

10. Devastated by their defeat in the 1999 European Cup final, a vengeful **Bayern Munich** beat United home and away the next time the clubs met in 2001.

11. United's only defeat during the successful 1968 European Cup wining campaign was against **Gornik Zabrze** in Poland. United didn't win a single away game en route to the Wembley final, drawing the three others

— YOU MUST HAVE COME IN A TAXI —

Stoke City brought 21,000 fans to Old Trafford for an FA Cup third round tie in 1967, in a crowd of 63,500. It remains the largest away following for a game at Old Trafford. The Stoke fans returned to the Potteries disappointed as United won 2–0.

— ALL CHANGE IN THE WAR —

During the Second World War, United used over 170 players in 260 wartime games. Jack Warner had the best appearance record, with 215.

— NOT SINGING (MUCH) ANY MORE? —

Less frequent celebrity visitors to Old Trafford:

Mick Hucknall: Purveyor of middle-of-the-road, ginger soul. He was allowed to train with United before the 4–0 defeat to Barcelona in 1994, leading one player to ask, "Is this a f*****g circus?"

Ed O'Brien: Radiohead's Red, who checks results whilst touring.

Zoe Ball: She's got a portrait of Eric Cantona in her Brighton front room.

Simon Le Bon: The Duran Duran singer struggled to get into the post-match players' party in Barcelona '99. Having wife Yasmin on his arm saw him in though.

Ulrika Jonsson: She used a game at Old Trafford to practise her Swedish on Sven Goran Eriksson.

Bertie Ahern: The Irish taoiseach is a Red.

Martin McGuiness: The Northern Irish politician.

Morrissey: Urmston born, Stretford bred. He was a Red. Is he now? He probably doesn't know himself.

Davy Jones: The former Monkee from Manchester. Now living in LA.

Tim Burgess: Another LA-based Red. Brian McClair is a big fan of this Charlatan.

Peter Noone: Herman's Hermits front man who sold 50 million records. Guess which US state starting 'Ca' he lives in?

— GETTING THE CHEQUEBOOK OUT —

Record English transfer fees paid by United:

Player	Fee	From	Date
Albert Quixall	£45,000	Sheffield Wednesday	September 1958
Denis Law	£115,000	Torino	August 1962
Willie Morgan	£117,000	Burnley	August 1968
Gordon McQueen	£450,000	Leeds United	February 1978
Bryan Robson	£1,500,000	West Brom	October 1981
Gary Pallister	£2,300,000	Middlesbrough	August 1989
Roy Keane	£3,750,000	Nottingham Forest	July 1993
Andy Cole	£7,000,000	Newcastle United	January 1995
Ruud van Nistelrooy	£19,000,000	PSV Eindhoven	July 2001
Juan Sebastian Veron	£28,100,000	Lazio	July 2001
Rio Ferdinand	£29,000,000	Leeds United	July 2002

— 'IT'S FOR CHARRIDDY' —

United have played in 23 Charity/Community Shields, including the 2007 victory over Chelsea at the new Wembley and the first ever one in 1908, winning 12, drawing four and losing seven. Here are some more interesting facts:

- In April 1908, the inaugural FA Charity Shield match was played between title winners United and Southern League champions QPR at Stamford Bridge. The match ended in a 1–1 draw. The replay, which United won 4–0, did not take place until the following August. The crowd for the first game was a mere 6,000, while 45,000 watched the replay.
- Willie Anderson was United's first official substitute, in the 1967 FA Charity Shield against Tottenham. The match ended in a 3–3 draw and is remembered for a remarkable goal scored by Spurs goalkeeper Pat Jennings, who launched a huge kick downfield which bounced over Alex Stepney's head and into the net.
- United have played Everton twice in the FA Charity Shield, losing both times: 4–0 at Goodison in 1963 and 2–0 at Wembley in 1985.
- Dennis Irwin made his debut for United at Wembley, in the 1990 Charity Shield against Liverpool.

— BEST-SELLERS —

The best-selling items in the Manchester United Megastore at Old Trafford are:

1. Replica shirts
2. Stationery – especially the three-pack of pens
3. Car accessories
4. United chocolate bars
5. Club crested keyrings
6. United cameras
7. Scarves
8. Hats
9. Player mugs
10. Plush toys
11. Footballs

— ER, NO THANKS! —

Eleven product ideas politely declined by the Megastore:

1. United toilet roll
2. United condoms
3. United coffins
4. United toilet seats
5. United garters
6. United hub caps
7. United paving stones
8. United blow-up dolls
9. United cat flaps
10. United plasters
11. United edible knickers

— FULL-BACK RECORD —

The £10,000 paid to United by Preston in December 1948, for Joe Walton, was a record for a full-back at the time. Walton, although only making 23 appearances for United, played for England against Scotland in the Burnden Park Disaster Fund match. He was also a member of the Accrington Stanley side who went out of the Football League in March 1962.

— GROUND FULL —

The top ten all-time season's highest average attendances of English clubs:

Club	Season	Average
Manchester United	2006/07	75,898
Manchester United	2005/06	69,374
Manchester United	2004/05	67,644
Manchester United	2003/04	67,641
Manchester United	2002/03	67,630
Manchester United	2001/02	67,586
Manchester United	2000/01	67,544
Manchester United	1999/00	58,017
Manchester United	1967/68	57,552
Newcastle United	1947/48	56,283

— HEATHENS ON A ROLL —

In season 1894/95, Newton Heath scored 14 goals in successive home fixtures. On April 3rd the Heathens defeated Walsall Town Swifts 9–0 and on April 6th Newcastle United 5–1. This was bettered in season 1898/99 when they scored 15 in two games – winning 9–0 v Darwen on December 24th 1898 and 6–1 v Gainsborough Trinity on December 31st.

The following season, 1895/96, the Heathens scored five goals in each of three successive home fixtures: beating Liverpool 5–2 on November 2nd 1895, drawing 5–5 with Lincoln City on November 16th and beating Woolwich Arsenal 5–1 on November 30th.

Date	Result
Jan 2nd	Blackburn Rovers 4 Newton Heath 0 (FA Cup)
Jan 7th	Stoke City 7 Newton Heath 1
Jan 14th	Newton Heath 1 Nottingham Forest 3
Jan 26th	Newton Heath 0 Notts County 4
Feb 11th	Derby County 5 Newton Heath 1
Mar 4th	Newton Heath 0 Sunderland 5

— THE FINEST: TEN CRUCIAL RED MOMENTS —

1. The Treble

May 26th 1999. Manchester United become the first and so far only English club to win the European Cup, Premiership and FA Cup treble. Every Red cherishes their memories of those incredible last few minutes in Barcelona. Well, except George Best, who walked out of the Camp Nou because he thought Bayern Munich had done enough to beat United. Best didn't reckon on the indomitable spirit and resolve of Fergie's eleven, nor Teddy Sheringham or Ole Gunnar Solskjaer's extended toe.

2. European glory, May 29th 1968

Ten years after the Munich disaster, United become the first English club to win the European Cup. At the celebratory party in London's Russell Hotel, Matt Busby sings Louis Armstrong's 'It's A Wonderful World' while standing on a table. Afterwards, when asked whether he is thinking of the fallen Munich team at that point, he says, "Deep down the sorrow is there all the time. It becomes part of you."

Bobby Charlton prefers a more literal, rather than emotional response. Asked by a journalist, "How does it feel to lift the trophy ten years after walking from the Munich wreckage?" he answers, "bloody heavy."

The spirit of '68

3. J.H. Davies saves the club, 1902

Newton Heath are declared bankrupt when businessman John Henry Davies, the managing director of Manchester Breweries, is persuaded to invest money into the club by fundraisers who include the players.

Later chairman, Davies oversees the name change to Manchester United and pays for the new stadium to be built at Old Trafford in 1910. His death, in 1927, heralds the most desperate period in United's history.

4. The 1990s doubles: 1994 and 1996

Although achieved with two very different sides, the 90s league and cup doubles illustrate United's dominance of the English domestic game. The 1994 side is quick, wily and hard; the 1996 team stuffed with hungry young homespun prodigies. That the doubles are achieved with cup final victories over Chelsea and Liverpool enhances their value. If only United could have made it another double in 2007.

5. Louis Rocca writes to Matt Busby, December 15th 1944

Rocca, United's assistant manager and chief scout, has been trying to trace Busby for a month as the Second World War comes to a close. They didn't have hotmail in 1944. Worried about sending it to Liverpool – Busby's previous employers – Rocca writes a slightly conspiratorial letter to the Busby family home in which he said talks of "having a great job for you". He implores Busby to get in touch with him at Old Trafford. Busby obliges, and is Manchester United manager for the next quarter of a century.

6. United sign Sir Alex Ferguson, November 1986

How and where he signed remains disputed, but the decision to tempt Ferguson from Aberdeen to replace Ron Atkinson remains former chairman Martin Edwards' most astute move. Ferguson had turned down the jobs at Tottenham and Arsenal, but having once heard his mentor Jock Stein tell him how he regretted turning down the United job in 1971, Ferguson doesn't make the same mistake. Implausibly, Ferguson's first contract at Old Trafford pays him less than he was on at Aberdeen.

7. Victory in the 1948 FA Cup final

The win is United's first trophy in almost 40 years. Blackpool lead twice, and hold out until the 70th minute, when Busby's first great side blitzes the Seasiders 4–2 at Wembley. Illustrating how far United's stock had fallen in the previous decades, United regain their role as the pre-eminent Manchester club for the first time since the end of the First World War.

8. 1977 FA Cup Final
"We stopped Liverpool winning the treble," says United's first goalscorer Stuart Pearson of the cup final win over Liverpool. "We'd lost the cup a year earlier and didn't want to feel like that again. But we were not too confident. We knew we'd give Liverpool a game, but they were so good that you could never say: 'Right, we're going to beat these today.'" But beat them United did, 2–1.

9. Rotterdam, May 15th 1991
Ferguson's first European trophy with United, as the Catalans are vanquished 2–1 in the European Cup Winners' Cup final. Reds outnumber Barça fans in the Rotterdam rain, singing along to the Madchester anthems of the time like 'Sit Down' by James. After the five-year ban on English clubs, United's success means that the club are again mentioned as 'European giants' for the first time since the 1960s.

10. Arsenal 4 Manchester United 5, February 1st 1958
The final game the Busby Babes play on English soil and arguably their finest ever performance. United are unstoppable. Three up at half-time, the Babes produce an overall performance that proves beyond doubt to the cynical London media that Busby's side are the greatest post-war English club side. The chance of a third consecutive championship lies ahead. But so does a trip to Belgrade.

— WE'LL MEET AGAIN —

United's most frequent opponents in all competitions:

Total games	Club
200	Arsenal
172	Everton
172	Liverpool
166	Aston Villa
162	Tottenham Hotspur
148	Manchester City
147	Newcastle United
146	Chelsea
124	Sheffield Wednesday
121	Sunderland

— TERRACE CLASSICS —

More cult chants from the Stretford End:

*'I see the Stretford End arising, I see the trouble on the way, Don't go
out tonight, if you don't wear red and white, 'Cos I've seen the
Stretford Enders fight'*
(To the tune of Creedence Clearwater Revival's 'Bad Moon Rising')

*'From the banks of the River Irwell, to the shores of Sicily,
We will fight, fight, fight for United, 'til we win the Football League,
To hell with Liverpool, to hell with Man City (they're s**t!),
We will fight, fight, fight for United, 'til we win the Football League'*
(To the 'Sousa March')

*'Bertie Mee said to Don Revie, "Have you heard of the North Bank,
Highbury?"*
*"No" said Matt, "you cockney t**t, but he's heard of the Stretford
Enders."'*
(To 'A Nice Cockney Lilt')

*'Bobby gets the ball on the centre spot, passes it to Georgie on the wing,
Georgie beats his man and puts in a cross for Denis Law, And it's a
goal, And he's the king.*
Ob-la-di, Ob-la-da, Man United, European Champions'
(The Beatles' influence at Old Trafford)

*'Who put the ball in the Germans' net? Who put the ball in the
Germans' net? Who put the ball in the Germans' net? Ole Gunnar
Solskjaer.'*
**(Celebrating the 1999 Champions League Final win over Bayern
Munich)**

*'What do you want to go to Wembley for?
Take a trip down Oldham Road, And you're in Ireland,
Take a walk down Ancoats Lane, And you're in Italy grand,
China and Japan in Upper Brook Street,
Greengate and you're in Alabam,
And if you keep walking still,
Palestine's in Cheetham Hill,
So what do you wanna go to Wembley for?
To see United!'*

'*C'mon without, c'mon within, you aint seen nothing like the mighty Wyn*'
(Despite only playing 16 times for United, Wyn Davies had his own song, sung to the tune of 'The Mighty Quinn' by Manfred Mann)

'*Oh I'd like to know where Rush got his nose from?*'
(United fans ask the obvious question about Ian Rush. To the tune of 'Rock the Boat' by the Hues Corporation)

'*Oh Manchester, Manchester United,*
A bunch of bouncing Busby Babes,
They deserve to be knighted.
Whenever they're playing in your town, be sure to get to that football ground,
Take a lesson, come and see,
The football taught by Matt Busby,
Oh, Manchester, Manchester United, a bunch of bouncing Busby babes, they deserve to be knighted . . .'

— 'WE'RE TAKIN' OVER BARCELONA' —

The ten biggest United away followings (excluding domestic cup finals and semi-finals):

United fans	Total crowd	Stadium	Occasion
55,000	90,000	Barcelona, May 1999	Champions League final
26,000	45,000	Rotterdam, May 199	ECWC final
25,000	30,115	Wimbledon, May 1993	Premiership
25,000	38,152	Bolton, March 1975	Division Two
19,000	26,384	Oldham, December 1974	Division Two
18,000	48,105	Sheff Wed, November 1985	Division One
17,000	25,370	Blackpool, October 1974	Division Two
17,000	54,161	Arsenal, February 1988	FA Cup fifth round
16,000	44,184	Chelsea, May 1973	Division One
13,000	21,055	Notts Cty, January 1992	Division One

— THE DOC —

In July 1977, just two months after guiding United to victory in the FA Cup over arch-rivals and soon-to-be European Champions Liverpool, Tommy Docherty was sacked as Manchester United manager. Docherty, married with three children, was shown the door after revelations that he had been having an affair with the wife of club physiotherapist Laurie Brown.

"I have been punished for falling in love."
Tommy Docherty, after being sacked.

"The thing that got him sacked wasn't the falling in love – it was making the physio reserve team manager, sending him out on scouting trips and giving his wife one while he was away."
Willie Morgan

"I am biased where Tommy [Docherty] is concerned and I make no apology for it. To me, the man is magic."
Willie Morgan, while Docherty was United manager. The pair later fell out, their acrimony leading to an appearance in court at The Old Bailey.

"I gave the club the FA Cup. They gave me the sack."
Tommy Docherty

"Managers are honest, marvellous people a lot of the time. But we all tell lies. Any manager who is not honest enough to admit that is the biggest liar of them all."
Tommy Docherty

"Football management these days is like nuclear war – no winners, just survivors."
Tommy Docherty

"It will be all downhill from now on. Leaving Manchester United is like leaving the Hilton and booking at some run-down little hotel round the corner."
Tommy Docherty after Ron Atkinson was sacked in 1986

— THE WRONG SIDE OF THE LAW —

United's players (and management) have been involved in several high-profile brushes with authority over the years. Here is how various Reds have fought the law and, in some cases, won:

- **Eric Cantona:** The Frenchman originally received a two-week jail sentence from Mrs Jane Pearch, chairman of Croydon magistrates, after launching a kung fu kick at a Crystal Palace supporter during a match at Selhurst Park in January 1995. This was later commuted to 120 hours of community service. Cantona's team-mate Paul Ince was found not guilty of assault for his involvement in the affair.
- **Roy Keane:** The United skipper was arrested in May 1999 after a woman alleged he assaulted her in Mulligans, an Irish pub in Manchester, as United's players celebrated winning the first leg of the treble. Keane was released without charge. He later wrote, "It was a set-up, but that was no excuse. I was just a daft f****r."
- **Nicky Butt:** The midfielder was arrested by police in May 2003 after an incident in Brasingamens nightclub in Alderley Edge, Cheshire. As in Keane's case, assault was alleged but Butt was also found to have done nothing wrong and was not charged.
- **Cristiano Ronaldo:** Police questioned Ronaldo and another man in October 2005 over an alleged sexual assault. The Portugal winger denied the allegation and the Crown Prosecution Service stated that there was insufficient evidence to press charges.
- **George Best:** Over a decade after his United career had ended, the wayward genius was jailed for 12 weeks for drink-driving and assaulting a police officer. An appeal failed and Best spent Christmas 1984 in Pentonville prison, north London. Six years later, Best was bound over for assaulting a man in a London pub.
- **Sir Alex Ferguson:** In October 1999 the boss was cleared of driving his BMW on the hard shoulder of the M602 in Eccles after his solicitor successfully argued that Ferguson had an upset stomach and needed to use the toilet. In the same month, Ferguson was also cleared of speeding by Derby magistrates, as there was not sufficient proof that he was driving his car at the time.

— TOP OF THE PYRAMID —

United winger Danny Wallace scored on his England international debut against Egypt in 1986. He never pulled on the white shirt again.

— VISITING STARS —

The ten best opposing players seen at Old Trafford:

1. **Dejan Savicevic:** Star player for the European champions Red Star Belgrade, he played in the 1991 European Super Cup final at Old Trafford. "Anyone at that game must still be wondering how we won it," said Sir Alex. "I know I am. Savicevic was absolutely sensational." When Savicevic had to go off injured, the relief among the players was palpable.

2. **Fernando Redondo:** "Redondo's forward run and beautiful turn past Henning Berg was football of the highest class." That's what Roy Keane reckoned of Madrid's best player, the man who stopped United retaining the European Cup in 2000.

3. **Eric Cantona:** It's not often that the K-Stand applauds a visiting player, but the spontaneity which greeted an overhead kick by Eric Cantona of Leeds United in September 1992 was recognition of genius. Bruce and Pallister rushed to tell their manager the same. Two months later Cantona crossed the Pennines.

4. **Ronaldo:** The buck-toothed Brazilian scored a hat-trick in Real Madrid's 4–3 defeat at Old Trafford in April 2003. He was applauded off the field when substituted and said he felt "honoured by appreciation of the Manchester fans."

5. **Stefan Effenberg:** Bayern Munich's main man, he outclassed Keane in his prime as a vengeful Bayern beat United home and away in the 2001 Champions League.

6. **Marco van Basten:** Although he only appeared at Old Trafford in a 1988 friendly, the Dutch striker was the star at a time when Milan were football's Harlem Globetrotters while United averaged 38,000. They had Baresi, we had Colin Gibson; them, Gullit, us, Liam O'Brien; Milan, Frank Rijkaard, United, Graeme Hogg. You get the picture.

7. **Dennis Bailey:** An oddity, but like Ronaldo, he scored a hat-trick at Old Trafford, this one on New Year's Day 1992. Ronaldo's career fared better for Bailey managed just one more league goal in his QPR career.

8. **Edgar Davids** and **Zinedine Zidane:** Juve's 1999 midfield pairing completely dominated the European Cup semi-final at Old Trafford in 1999. A late Giggs goal gave United a barely deserved draw.

9. **Bryan Robson:** West Brom's Laurie Cunningham was the star, Cyrille Regis its speed, yet a young Robson bulldozed the Baggies to a 5–3 win at Old Trafford in December 1978.

10. Ricardo Izecson dos Santos Leite – **Kaka** to his mates – was the outstanding Milan player in the 2007 Champions League semi-final. The brilliant Brazilian scored twice in Milan's 3–2 defeat, his performance over two legs easily outshining that of Cristiano Ronaldo, United's hope for the 2007 European Footballer of the Year award.

— 'A CHEQUE WILL DO NICELY' —

United's biggest transfer sales:

Player	Fee	To	Date
Alan Gowling	£60,000	Huddersfield Town	June 1972
Ted MacDougall	£170,000	West Ham	March 1973
Gordon Hill	£275,000	Derby Country	April 1978
Brian Greenhoff	£350,000	Leeds United	August 1979
Andy Ritchie	£500,000	Brighton	October 1980
Ray Wilkins	£1,400,000	Milan	June 1984
Mark Hughes	£1,800,000	Barcelona	August 1986
Dion Dublin	£1,950,000	Coventry City	September 1994
Paul Ince	£6,000,000	Inter Milan	June 1995
Jaap Stam	£16,500,000	Lazio	September 2001
David Beckham	£25,000,000	Real Madrid	July 2003

— 'SCORE IN A BROTHEL . . .' —

United's lowest league top scorers in a season:

Season	Player	Goals
1972/73	Bobby Charlton	6
1973/74	Sammy McIlroy	6
1920/21	Three players	7
1933/34	Neil Dewar	8
1893/94	Alf Farman	8
1914/15	George Anderson	10
1978/79	Steve Coppell, Jimmy Greenhoff	11
1932/33	Bill Ridding	11
1906/07	George Wall	11
1902/03	Jack Peddie	11
1901/02	Steve Preston	11
1903/04	Three players	11

— WHAT A GAME! —

Ollie puts the ball in the Germans' net!

The top ten greatest United victories . . . ever!

1. **Manchester United 2 Bayern Munich 1**: May 26th 1999. Solskjaer and Sheringham's late, great, show.
2. **Manchester 4 Benfica 1**: May 29th 1968. Three injury time goals and United become the first English team to win the European Cup.
3. **Juventus 2 Manchester United 3**: April 21st 1999. The Roy Keane show. With support from Cole and Yorke at their finest.
4. **Benfica 1 Manchester United 5**: March 9th 1966. When George Best dazzled the Stadium of Light, leading the Portuguese press to name him 'El Beatle'.
5. **Manchester United 3 Barcelona 0**: March 21st 1984. The Catalans, with Maradona, won the first leg of this Cup Winners' Cup quarter-final 2–0. United stormed back and beat them 3–0 at Old Trafford. Many fans say it's the best atmosphere they've ever witnessed.
6. **United 2 Liverpool 1**: May 21st 1977. The Scousers were going for the treble and needed to beat United in the FA Cup final. They didn't.
7. **Arsenal 4 United 5**: February 1st 1958. The last game before Munich. And what a game.
8. **Manchester City 2 Newton Heath 5**: November 3rd 1894. The first Manchester derby. The pecking order was established from the start.
9. **United 10 Anderlecht 0**: September 26th 1956. The first European match to be played at Old Trafford and still the club's record victory.
10. **United 7 Roma 1**: April 10th 2007. The Italians came to Old Trafford with the best defence in the world's most defensive league. Backed by 3,800 fans, many wearing 'Invasion of Manchester' T-shirts, they slipped a goal behind. Then two, three, four . . .

— KOP THAT —

Between season 1978/79 and 1987/88, a dominant Liverpool lost just 19 league games at Anfield. Four of those were against United. In the 20 league fixtures between the two sides during the 1980s, when Liverpool won the league title five times and United didn't win it once, United lost just one game to Liverpool and won seven.

— ITALIAN JOBS —

- United have lost ten of their 13 competitive games in Italy. Their first victory came when they famously came back from a two goal first-half deficit to beat Juventus in the 1999 Champions League semi-final.
- United have played Milan three times in the semi-finals of the European Cup/Champions League, with the Italians winning on all three occasions. The first was in the aftermath of the 1958 Munich air disaster, the second in 1969 when United were holders, the third was in 2007 when Milan overcame a 3–2 deficit at Old Trafford to win 3–0 in the San Siro.
- The 7–1 win against Roma in the Champions League/European Cup was the second biggest in the tournament's quarter-final stage. Real Madrid's 8–0 victory over Seville in 1958 remains the biggest win in the last eight.

— SUMMER DAYS —

The latest United have ever played a game during a domestic season was on June 1st 1940 against Everton in the War Regional League (Western Division). Stanley Matthews played as a guest for United, but failed to inspire his new team-mates, as the Toffees won 3–0.

— LIMITED CAREER —

Paul Bielby appeared in the same England Youth team as Glenn Hoddle and former Reds Bryan Robson, Peter Barnes and Ray Wilkins, but he failed to reach similar heights as his former team-mates, making only two first team starts with United and a further two as substitute.

— SUPER MAC —

Sammy McIlroy made a playing 'comeback' with Northwich Victoria during his time as player-manager, two years after hanging up his boots. Matt Busby's last signing couldn't take the Vics out of the Conference but he has since led two other north-west non-league teams into the Football League, Macclesfield Town in 1997 and Morecambe a decade later.

— WEDDING BELLS —

Don Gibson, a United half-back, married Matt Busby's daughter, while Tommy Bogan, a forward, married his niece.

— INFLATED FEE —

United signed Harry Rowley for £100 in May 1928 from Shrewsbury Town. They re-signed him in December 1934 from Oldham Athletic for £1,375.

— BEARDSLEY BOOB —

Possibly the biggest transfer boob in the club's history was Ron Atkinson allowing Peter Beardsley, a £300,000 signing from Vancouver Whitecaps in 1982, to return to the Canadian club, having played only half a game – a Football League Cup tie against Bournemouth. Beardsley went on to have a notable career with Newcastle, Liverpool and England, playing almost 1,000 games and scoring over 270 goals.

Beardsley's brother-in-law Shaun is a United fan who always refused free tickets, preferring to stand in his usual spot in the Stretford End. Shaun still watches United home and away.

— HARDMAN OF ALL TRADES —

Former United director and chairman Harold Hardman played for the club as an amateur on four occasions during the 1908/09 season. He was an England international at both full and amateur level, and also gained FA Cup winners and runners-up medal with Everton in 1906 and 1907 respectively. While representing Great Britain in the 1908 Olympic Games football tournament he added a gold medal to his trophy cabinet.

— PROUD HERO —

Onetime United winger George Mutch became a cup final hero with Preston North End, scoring a last minute extra-time penalty against Huddersfield Town in the 1938 Wembley final. With the game goalless, Mutch was brought down inside the box by a Huddersfield defender. After prolonged treatment, he took the spot-kick himself, his shot going in off the underside of the crossbar. He later admitted that he could remember little about it.

— PINING FOR THE FJORDS —

When United's 1968 European Cup winner Tony Dunne took over as manager of Norwegian club Stenjker, he replaced his former United team-mate Bill Foulkes.

— WHITE AND RED ROSES —

Twelve players who played for both United and Leeds, other than Eric Cantona:

Joe Jordan, Gordon McQueen, Alan Smith, Arthur Graham, Dennis Irwin, Lee Sharpe, Brian Greenhoff, Andy Ritchie, Freddie Goodwin, Gordon Strachan, Mickey Thomas and David Healy.

— LIKE A GREASY CHIP BUTTY —

Lou Macari, who had a fish and chip shop outside Old Trafford, was not the first United player to be associated with such an enterprise. Sixties winger John Connelly owned a similar outlet in Brierfield, near Burnley. Unlike Macari, Connelly could be found behind the counter frying away and serving customers.

— DREAM DEBUTS —

Neil Webb only scored 11 goals for United, but managed a unique record of scoring on his debut in the First Division, FA Cup, League Cup and European Cup Winners' Cup.

— MILAN . . . OVERLAND —

Having defeated Red Star Belgrade prior to the Munich air disaster in 1958, United faced AC Milan in the semi-final of the European Cup. The second leg in Milan created something of a dilemma for United officials as the team understandably did not wish to fly so soon after the traumatic crash. Instead, United travelled by boat and train, taking two days to arrive at their destination. Here are the full details of the trip from the club's official itinerary:

Saturday May 10th:	1.00pm: Report Old Trafford
	2.00pm: Depart London Road Station
	5.54pm: Arrive London Euston
Sunday May 11th:	10.15am: Depart Lancaster Court Hotel
	11.00am: Depart London Victoria Station
	1.00pm: Depart Dover
	2.20pm: Arrive Calais
	2.42pm: Depart Calais (by train)
Monday May 12th:	8.20am: Arrive Milan
Friday May 16th	5.22pm: Depart Milan
Saturday May 17th:	7.25am: Arrive Paris
	12.15pm: Depart Calais
	4.05pm: Arrive London Victoria
	6.00pm: Depart London Euston
	9.40pm: Arrive Manchester London Road

— FAMILY AFFAIR —

John McCartney, who made 20 appearances with Newton Heath during 1894/95, became manager of Heart of Midlothian in 1910. He was replaced by his son William in 1919. William died in 1948 and soon after, Matt Busby, who had played under William while guesting for Hibernian during the Second World War, took United to Easter Road to play in a benefit match for William's widow.

— CELTIC, UNITED . . . —

Forward George Livingstone not only played for both Manchester United (1908–14) and Manchester City, he also played for Rangers and Celtic north of the border.

— LATE TO LEICESTER —

In November 1902, the United players travelling by train to play Leicester Fosse were delayed due to a derailment at Nottingham. They subsequently had to get changed on the train. With the game kicking off late, there was no half-time interval and the match finished in semi-darkness.

— BILLY THE SCAPEGOAT —

Goalkeeper William Douglas was suspended by the Newton Heath directors following a poor display in the 5–2 defeat by Fairfield in the Manchester Cup. The club trainer was also dismissed.

— IT'S A FIX! —

On Good Friday 1915, United defeated Liverpool 2–0 at Old Trafford. Something of a surprise result, as United were battling against relegation and the visitors had been in good form. A few days after the match a letter appeared in the press, signed 'Football King', claiming that the match had been 'fixed'.

The football authorities launched an investigation into the matter and four Liverpool players and three United – Sandy Turnbull, Arthur Whalley and Enoch 'Knocker' West – were found guilty of match-fixing and banned for life.

It was later claimed that the players had met to plot the fixing of the game in the Dog and Partridge pub which stood close to the current popular match day watering hole, the Bishop Blaze. All were pardoned after the end of the Second World War (Turnbull died at Arras), apart from West who contested the verdict and protested his innocence. His ban was finally lifted in December 1945 – when he was 62!

— HEATHEN CENTURION —

Bob Parkinson scored Newton Heath's last goal of the 19th century and their first in the 20th. He only scored seven in his entire United career.

— HORACE'S CHAINS OF OFFICE —

Former United and Wales full-back Horace Blew was made Mayor of Wrexham in 1923.

— THE FIRST TESTIMONIAL —

John Aston senior was the first post-war United player to receive a testimonial. On April 25th 1956, United played an All-Star XI at Old Trafford. A versatile individual, Aston senior could play comfortably as a full back and as a centre forward, scoring 15 goals in 22 appearances as a striker during season 1950/51.

— HAT-TRICK IN VAIN —

Jackie Cape must be one of the few players ever to score a hat-trick yet still end up on the losing side. Cape scored three for United against Newcastle United at Old Trafford on September 20th 1930, but the Magpies hit back with seven.

— THE RED WOLF —

One of the top pre-war managers in the English game was Frank Buckley, who made three appearances with United. As a manager, he guided Wolverhampton Wanderers to the League Championship in 1938 and 1939 as well as a FA Cup final appearance in 1939. During the First World War, he was in the army and achieved the rank of Major, a title which remained with him during his managerial career.

— BETWEEN THE STICKS —

- Brian Greenhoff is one of a number of United outfield players who have stood in as a replacement goalkeeper. Others include John O'Shea, Jackie Blanchflower, Johnny Carey, Paddy Kennedy and Duncan Edwards.
- Wayne Rooney loves playing in goal during training and, although his team mates would not tell him, is actually quite good. Perhaps his lack of height has limited Sir Alex Ferguson from trying him in a first team game.
- Long-serving club secretary Les Olive played two games in goal for United, making his debut against Newcastle away in 1953 as all United's regular 'keepers were injured. United won 2–1 and Olive played against West Brom a week later at Old Trafford in a 2–2 draw.

— THE LAST HEATHEN —

The last player signed before Newton Heath changed their name to Manchester United was James Higson from Manchester Wednesday on April 28th 1902.

— A GOOD START —

Johnny Anderson became the first post-war player to appear in a FA Cup final (v Blackpool in 1948) and claim a winners' medal in the same season as he made his league debut.

— BETTER LUCK NORTH OF THE BORDER —

Frank Kopel won nothing with United during his five-year spell with the club. Upon returning to his native Scotland with Dundee United, following a spell with Blackburn Rovers, he won Scottish League Cup winners medals in 1980 and 1981 and a Scottish Cup runners' up medal in 1974 and 1981.

— OVER 30 YEARS A RED —

Former United assistant trainer Bill Inglis made 14 appearances for the club between 1926 and 1930. He returned to Old Trafford in 1934, remaining there until his role was taken over by Wilf McGuinness in 1961.

— THE BISHOP AUCKLAND CONNECTION —

Jack Allen, who joined United in May 1904, scoring two goals on his debut against Port Vale on September 3rd of that year, had appeared in two FA Amateur Cup Finals for his previous club Bishop Auckland. The north-east side also supplied United with Warren Bradley, who had also won FA Amateur Cup medals. Bradley joined United as an amateur in 1958 following Munich and by the end of the season had won full England international honours.

— BAD BET —

George Anderson, who made 86 appearances for United between 1911 and 1916, was jailed for eight months in 1918 following serious accusations of fraud in relation to betting on football matches.

— MASSIVE DIFFERENCE —

On the day City attracted a record crowd of 84,569 for their FA Cup quarter-final tie against Stoke City on March 3rd 1934, only 11,176 fans were at Old Trafford for United's Second Division fixture against Bury.

— YORKSHIRE IRE —

During United's promotion winning season of 1905/06, the team recorded a 5–1 victory at Bradford City on Feb 10th 1906. The locals were not happy and attacked United full-back Bob Bonthron as he left the dressing-room after the game.

— A GOAL FROM A THROW —

United were involved in possibly the only known instance of a goal being scored direct from a throw in. On January 22nd 1938, in an FA Cup tie at Barnsley, a long throw into the United goalmouth was touched into the net by goalkeeper Tommy Breen. United drew the game 2–2, but won the replay 1–0.

— HE FEELS GOOD —

Former United forward James Brown, who played for the club between 1932 and 1934, played in the United States prior to his move to Old Trafford, having emigrated as a 17-year-old. He played in the 1930 World Cup for the States, scoring the only goal in their 6–1 quarter-final defeat by Argentina in Montevideo.

Brown was signed by United whilst on board the liner *Caledonia* before he arrived in England, United officials having boarded the ship in Ireland knowing that other clubs were interested.

— USA REDS —

Ten Manchester United players, other than David Beckham, who later went to play in north America:

Ian Storey-Moore (Chicago Sting)
Dennis Viollet (Baltimore Bays)
Alex Stepney (Dallas Tornado)
David Sadler (Miami Toros)
Jimmy Ryan (Dallas Tornado)
Willie Anderson (Portland Timbers)
Jimmy Kelly (Chicago Sting, LA Aztecs, Tulsa Roughnecks, Toronto Blizzard)
Gordon Hill (Chicago Sting, NY Arrows, Kansas Comets)
George Best (LA Aztecs, Fort Lauderdale Strikers, San Jose Earthquakes)
Tony Dunne (Detroit Express)

— NUMBER 41 REPLACES NUMBER 38 —

Although football today is based around a squad system, it is unlikely that United will ever use the same number of players that they did in wartime football:

Season	Players used
1915/16	39
1916/17	41
1917/18	39
1918/19	39
1939/40	38
1940/41	39
1941/42	32
1942/43	39
1943/44	39
1944/45	39

— SEVEN WINS THEN THE SACK —

United finished season 1980/81 with a run of seven consecutive wins, four of them 1–0, but it was not enough to prevent manager Dave Sexton from getting the sack in the summer. United fans were not happy with the style of football under Sexton, which they perceived to be unadventurous.

— BUSY BAILEY —

Goalkeeper Gary Bailey saved three penalties against Ipswich Town at Portman Road on March 1st 1980 – one from Frans Thijssen and a twice taken attempt by Kevin Beattie – but United still lost 6–0. The Portman Road side would probably have claimed the result as revenge for United's 5–0 victory at Old Trafford in April 1962, a week or so before Ipswich were crowned league champions.

Bailey had made his debut against Ipswich Town in November 1978, the side that his father Roy had played for in the 1960s.

— EIGHT ACE —

Jack Rowley, a striker for United before and after the Second World War, scored all Wolverhampton Wanderers' goals in their 8–1 war-time victory over Derby County in February 1944.

— RESERVES PROSPER —

On April 22nd 1957, Matt Busby made nine changes to the United side who had beaten Sunderland two days previously, because of an impending European Cup semi-final tie on the Wednesday. Despite the changes, United defeated Burnley with what was basically a reserve team 2–0. The United juniors, promoted to the reserves, also defeated the Turf Moor side.

— FIRST INTERNATIONAL —

The first ever international match played at Old Trafford in 1926, saw England beat Scotland 1–0.

— FAN PROTESTS —

In October 1930, 3,000 United fans turned up at Hulme Town Hall to protest at the club's form. United were bottom of the league having not picked up a point in their first ten games of the season. Fans decided to boycott the game against Arsenal the following day and just 23,406 showed up – well down on the 50,000 that would have usually attend the fixture. United lost 2–1 and were relegated at the end of the season.

— ONLY A GAME —

Ten players who only ever played one game for United:

1. **Jimmy Davis:** The talented winger played in the 4–0 League Cup defeat at Arsenal in 2001. He then spent two years on loan at Swindon and Watford. Tragically, Davis died in a car accident on the M40 in 2003.

2. **Nick Culkin:** The man with the shortest United career, the goalkeeper replaced Raimond van der Gouw for the final 18 seconds in a 2–1 victory at Arsenal in 1999.

3. **Pat McGibbon:** Not only was his only game the 3–0 home defeat to York City in 1995, but the Ulsterman also experienced the ignominy of being sent off.

4. **Tony Hawksworth:** A lance-corporal in the Tank Regiment, he received a call at work asking him to play in goal for United at Blackpool that afternoon in October 1956. United drew 2–2.

5. **Colin McKee:** A member of the 1992 FA Youth Cup winning side, the Glaswegian winger played 75 minutes in the celebratory final game of the 1993/94 season.

6. **Dennis Walker:** The first black player to wear red, the Northwich-born forward played in a weakened pre-FA Cup final team against Forest in May 1963. United lost 3–2.

7. **'Anto' Whelan:** A Dubliner who covered for injured compatriot Kevin Moran in a home game against Southampton in 1980.

8. **Harold Bratt:** He played in front of the lowest post-war United crowd when Bradford City beat United 2–1 in 1960's inaugural League Cup.

9. **Richard Wellens:** Wore red for just 16 minutes in a 3–0 League Cup defeat to Aston Villa in 1999.

10. **Jonathan Clark:** Waited three years for his debut. When it came he gave the ball away with one of his first touches against Sunderland at Old Trafford in October 1976. The Mackems equalised.

— S-A-L-F-O-R-D —

- In 1958, Salford rugby league club hired Old Trafford to experiment with playing a game under floodlights. Over 8,000 watched them beat Leeds.

- Salford had been given the 'Red Devils' nickname before United after a French newspaper called them 'Les Diables Rouges' following a game in France in the 1960s.

- Billy Garton, the Salford-born defender who played 50 games from the club in the 1980s, held his testimonial game at Salford after United refused to let him have one at Old Trafford. Garton was forced to retire after suffering chronic fatigue syndrome.

— RED HEAVYWEIGHTS —

1.	Peter SchmeicheL	15st 13lb
2.	Gary Pallister	14st 13lb
3.	Gary Walsh	14st 13lb
4.	Jaap Stam	14st 1lb
5.	Mark Bosnich	13st 7lb
6.	Gary Bailey	13st 12lb
7.	Eric Cantona	13st 11lb
8.	Gordon Clayton	13st 9lb
9.	Les Sealey	13 lb 8lb
10.	Alex Dawson	13st 6lb
11=	Paul McGrath	13st 5lb
11=	Jim Holton	13st 5lb

— TV DEBUTS —

The 1952 Charity Shield between title winners United and FA Cup winners Newcastle was shown live on BBC television, yet the Beeb only covered 50 minutes of the game. Luckily for the cameras, they caught five of the game's six goals as the Geordies were vanquished 4–2.

— SHOPPING BASKETS —

In 1985, United considered building a 9,000 seater indoor arena on the number one car park, opposite Old Trafford, to house the Manchester United basketball team. Martin Edwards had visions of a Barcelona-style sports club. Unfortunately, he didn't have the money to fund it and the car park remained in use on Sundays as a market.

— SHALOM —

The first non-European team to visit Old Trafford were Hapoel Tel Aviv for a friendly in September 1951. United beat the Israelis 6–0 in a game watched by just 12,000. Red Star Belgrade had been the first foreign team to visit four months earlier as part of the Festival of Britain celebrations.

— LANDMARK FERGIE GOALS —

Peter Schmeichel scores United's 760th goal under Fergie

United have scored over 2,000 goals in competitive games during Sir Alex Ferguson's management. Here are some of the most important and the most memorable:

No.	Date	Competition	Venue	Goalscorer
1	November 22nd 1986	Division One	Old Trafford	John Sivebaek v QPR
217	January 7th 1990	FA Cup	City Ground	Mark Robins v Nottingham Forest
500	April 17th 1993	Premiership	Old Trafford	Eric Cantona v Chelsea

760	September 26th 1995	UEFA Cup	Old Trafford	Peter Schmeichel v Rotor Volgograd
844	August 17th 1996	Premiership	Selhurst Park	David Beckham v Wimbledon
1,000	January 4th 1998	FA Cup	Stamford Bridge	Andy Cole v Chelsea
1,144	April 14th 1999	FA Cup	Villa Park	Ryan Giggs v Arsenal
1,162	May 26th 1999	Champions Lge	Nou Camp	Ole Gunnar Solskjaer v Bayern Munich
1,500	March 30th 2002	Premiership	Elland Road	Ole Gunnar Solskjaer v Leeds
2,000	December 23rd 2006	Premiership	Villa Park	Cristiano Ronaldo v Aston Villa

— A LITTLE RESPECT —

Just 7,000 Reds showed up for the 1992 testimonial for 1980s terrace hero Norman Whiteside. Unfortunately for the Ulsterman, the game came a week after United had blown the league title and fans were not in charitable mood. It was also the last ever game at which fans were able to stand on the Stretford End.

— SHORT REDS —

Terry Gibson	1985–1987	5ft 4in
Ernest Taylor	1957–1959	5ft 4in
Danny Wallace	1989–1993	5ft 5in
Herbert Burgess	1906–1910	5ft 5in
Henry Cockburn	1946–1954	5ft 5in
Gordon Strachan	1984–1989	5ft 5in
Steve Coppell	1975–1983	5ft 6in
Jesper Olsen	1984–1989	5ft 6in
Nobby Stiles	1960–1971	5ft 6in
Johnny Giles	1959–1963	5ft 6in
Remi Moses	1981–1988	5ft 6in

— RED BOOZERS —

The Trafford: Situated at the top of Sir Matt Busby Way, it is the closest pub to Old Trafford. Normally where news crews go to source a Red fan opinion from someone with a Manchester accent.

The Bishop Blaze: Want to sing songs about City, Scousers and Leeds on a loop? In conditions similar to a Turkish steam bath? Join the queue outside.

The Quadrant, Stretford: Close to the Lancashire cricket ground, this was a favoured hangout of the Busby Babes, many of whom had lodgings nearby. Tommy Taylor had an understanding with the publican who would quietly refill his glass under the counter with gin while he had a bottle of tonic on the table.

The Peveril of the Peak: Eric Cantona was known to call into this wonderful Victorian pub for a pint and a game of table football. Against the well-practised regulars, he didn't quite make the impact on a table football that he made on a real pitch.

Best's hangouts: Best was a regular in Manchester's clubs and pubs in the 1960s and 1970s. He drank in the Brown Bull pub near Salford Crescent, and Blinkers, an intimate basement club with coved seating on Bridge Street with his team-mates Jimmy Ryan, David Sadler and John Fitzpatrick. Annabelle's on Brazenoze Street was another favoured Best haunt, and he later became a partner in the Slack Alice club. All have now either closed or changed names.

The Gorse Hill: Big Victorian pub on the A56 in Stretford. Popular with supporters' club branches on match days.

Sam Platts: Modern pub overlooking the Manchester Ship canal and Salford Quays.

The Tollgate: Modern pub opposite Trafford Bar Metro Station – the one before Old Trafford. Always busy pre-match with Reds.

The White Lion, Castlefield: United memorabilia adorns the wall of this boozer on Liverpool Road. The Red landlord also organises barges to home games from outside. Try it.

The Living Room: The discreet top floor of this Deansgate bar is where several United players like to chill. Although it's so dark you wonder how they can see each other.

— BEST LEAGUE SEASONS —

United's ten best seasons, by results*:

Season	P	W	D	L	F	A	Pts	%
1. 1999/00	38	28	7	3	97	45	63	82.8
2. 2006/07	38	28	5	5	83	27	61	80.2
2. 1993/94	42	27	11	4	80	38	65	77.3
3. 2002/03	38	25	8	5	74	34	58	76.3
4. 1956/57	42	28	8	6	103	54	64	76.1
5. 1998/99	38	22	13	3	80	37	57	75.0
6. 1995/96	38	25	7	6	73	35	57	75.0
7. 2000/01	38	24	8	6	79	31	56	73.6
8. 1964/65	42	26	9	7	89	39	61	72.6
9. 1966/67	42	24	12	6	84	45	60	71.4
10. 1992/93	42	24	12	6	67	31	60	71.4

* Table is devised using the old system of two points for a league win. Rankings are according to the total percentage of points gained. Goal difference is used to separate sides.

— AND THE WINNING NUMBER IS . . . —

Ten celebrities who have made the half-time cash dash draw at Old Trafford:

1. **Simon Le Bon** – if only wife Yasmin had joined him.
2. **'Posh' Spice** and **'Sporty' Spice** – when Victoria and David first swapped monosyllables.
3. **Sir Roger Moore** – a walk on the park for 007.
4. **Kevin Keegan** – Newcastle's then manager thought he was going to be drawing a raffle in a room, not the centre circle. He was booed for his troubles.
5. **Bernard Gallagher** – when everyone wanted his daughter Kirsty . . .
6. **Richard Branson** – never one to spurn some self promotion.
7. **Sir Rodney Black** – The stern Falklands Task Force commander. No 'Argentina' chants for him.
8. **Sam Torrance** – with that moustache he was mistaken for a Bolton fan.
9. **Peter Kay** – had Reds in stitches, despite having a pop at them.
10. **Richard Wilson** – Victor Meldrew did a reluctant turn.

— FOOTBALL'S FIRST SUPERSTAR —

Billy Meredith

Many players have played for both United and City, but few have served both with such with distinction as Billy Meredith, who won the FA Cup with both clubs. Born in Chirk, North Wales, Meredith was football's first superstar. He joined City in October 1894 and a week later scored two goals against Newton Heath in the first Manchester derby.

In 1904, amid allegations of bribery, he was hit with an 18-month ban. After serving this he moved to United in 1906 and quickly became a fans' favourite. In 1921 he returned to City where he continued playing until he was 49 – his last match against Newcastle in the semi-finals at the age of 49 years and 245 days makes him the oldest player ever to play in the FA Cup.

Meredith played 335 games for United, scoring 36 goals and winning two league championships, an FA Cup and two Charity Shields. He also played 390 times for City and scored 150 goals. He died in Withington, Manchester in 1958, aged 83.

— COME TO SEE THE KIDS —

A record 61,599 watched the two FA Youth Cup Final games between holders United and Leeds in 1993. A crowd of 30,562 watched the first leg at Old Trafford, 31,037 came to the second. Leeds won the competition.

— TEN APPALLING DEFEATS —

Score	Versus	Date
1. 0–7	Blackburn Rovers (a) Div 1	April 1926
2. 0–7	Aston Villa (a) Div 1	December 1930
3. 0–7	Wolves (a) Div 2	December 1931
4. 0–6	Leicester City (a) Div 1	March 1961
5. 0–6	Ipswich Town (a) Div 1	March 1980
6. 0–6	Aston Villa (h) Div 1	March 1914
7. 0–6	Huddersfield Town (h) Div 1	September 1930
8. 1–7	Burnley (a) FA Cup	February 1901
9. 1–7	Newcastle United (h) Div 1	September 1927
10. 2–7	Sheffield Wednesday (h) FA Cup	February 1961

— RIGHT-HAND MEN —

Assistant managers to Sir Alex Ferguson:

Years	Assistant	Post-United career
1986–91	Archie Knox	Joined Rangers as assistant manager
1991–98	Brian Kidd	Joined Blackburn Rovers as manager
1999–01	Steve McClaren	Joined Middlesbrough as manager
2001–02	Jim Ryan	Redeployed at club
2002–03	Carlos Queiroz	Joined Real Madrid as head coach
2004–04	Walter Smith	Temporary three-month appointment
2004–	Carlos Queiroz	Still whispering in Fergie's ear

— REDS ON PLASTIC —

United played on a plastic pitch for the first time against QPR at Loftus Road in 1984, drawing 1–1. The club's overall record at Loftus Road during the grassless era was – played eight, won two, drawn four, lost two.

— REVENGE IS SWEET —

United's three FA Cup wins in 1985, 1990 and 1994 all contained the same bizarre coincidence. In the third round tie in each of those years, United knocked out the team which had knocked them out of the competition in the previous year: Bournemouth in 1985, Nottingham Forest in 1990 and Sheffield United in 1994.

— NAME ON THE SHIRT —

The logos of three different companies have adorned United's famous red shirts, since shirt sponsorship was introduced in the early 1980s: Sharp Electronics (later simply Sharp), Vodafone, AIG.

The current four-year deal with AIG (American International Group), an insurance and financial services institution, was completed in 2006 for a fee of £56.5 million, making it the biggest shirt sponsorship deal in English football.

— REDS HERE, THERE AND EVERYWHERE —

Where the majority of United's 75 million 'fans' live according to the club's own MORI conducted poll:

1. China 23.6 m
2. UK 9.7m
3. South Africa 5.9m
4. Malaysia 3.5m
5. USA 3.2m
6. Australia 3.2m
7. Thailand 3.2m
8. Japan 2.3m
9. Poland 2.2m
10. Singapore 2.1m
11. Canada 1.4m

— WHAT A GOAL! —

A goal to put hairs on your chest!

The ten greatest United goals from the last 25 years:

1. Ryan Giggs v Arsenal (Villa Park), FA Cup semi-final replay, April 14th 1999
Giggs intercepted a pass from Patrick Vieira in his own half then commenced a mazy dribble through five Arsenal players before thundering a shot past David Seaman. His celebration exposed enough chest hair to make David Hasselhoff envious. United were through to the final, with Ferguson saying: "There is not a player in the world to touch Giggs in that form." Inspired by the misplaced pass which allowed the treble, United fans still sing: "Vieira, wooah, he gave Giggsy the ball, and Arsenal won f**k all."

2. Dennis Irwin v Wimbledon (a), FA Cup fifth round, February 20th 1994
Pallister to Giggs to Hughes to Cantona to Kanchelskis to Parker to
Keane to Ince to Cantona to Ince to Giggs to Irwin. Every touch was
greeted with an *olé* from the travelling Reds. Then Irwin played a
one-two with Ince before scuffing a shot into the corner of the goal.
The 1994 side at its all-for-one best.

3. Ruud van Nistelrooy v Fulham (h), Premiership, March 22nd 2003
A glorious solo effort and the second of his three goals, the Dutchman
picked up the ball inside his own half with his back to goal. He then
outran the Fulham midfield, feinted past Melville, then rolled the ball
past keeper Taylor before he'd barely had a chance to reduce the angle.

**4. Bryan Robson v Liverpool (Maine Road), FA Cup semi-final replay,
April 17th 1985**
A goal down at Maine Road, Robson swapped passes with Frank
Stapleton on the half way line before running towards the Liverpool goal.
The pursuing Scouse defenders seemed close, until Robson unleashed a
shot that flew past Bruce Grobbelaar into the top corner of the net.

5. Norman Whiteside v Everton (Wembley), FA Cup final, May 18th 1985
Down to ten men against champions Everton after Kevin Moran
became the first man to be sent off in an FA Cup final, United should
have been beaten. Yet the 78th minute expulsion spurred Atkinson's
men. In extra time Mark Hughes passed to Whiteside, who ran into
the area and steadied himself before curling a deceptive shot past
Neville Southall.

6. Mark Hughes v Oldham Athletic, FA Cup semi-final, April 9th 1994
With 46 seconds remaining, Oldham led. Then Brian McClair lobbed
a hopeful ball into the area. Hughes met it, hitting a powerful volley
into the top right corner before running, face contorted, to celebrate
in front of the United fans. Oldham manager Joe Royle described it
as a "stroke of genius." His United counterpart's preferred superlative
was "miracle".

7. David Beckham v Wimbledon (a), Premiership, August 17th 1996
The moment Beckham became A-list. Having seen Jordi Cruyff almost
chip the Wimbledon keeper from outside the box, Beckham thought
he'd do likewise from his own half. With a swing of a boot the ball
sailed high through the blue Croydon sky, eventually coming to earth
in the Wimbledon net.

8. Mark Hughes v Barcelona (Rotterdam), Cup Winners' Cup final, May 15th 1991
Maybe it was a fraction offside, but Hughes' second goal against Barcelona was one of his best, a fierce volley from an implausible angle that, according to Ferguson, "left their goalkeeper picking daises somewhere."

9. Eric Cantona v Sunderland (h), Premiership, December 21st 1996
Collecting the ball just inside the Makems' half, Eric outmanoeuvred two opponents before playing a one-two with Brian McClair. Cantona briefly looked up, before chipping the ball over advancing 'keeper Perez. Cantona stood motionless, hands on hips, surveying all around him.

10. Norman Whiteside v Arsenal (Villa Park), FA Cup semi-final, April 16th 1983
With the score tied at 1–1, Whiteside hit a fantastic long range volley to give United victory. A photo of the goal won the sports photograph of the year award for 1983.

11. Paul Scholes v Bradford City (a), Premiership, March 25th 2000
Goals against Bradford were never a problem, but none were as good as this. Beckham played an inch perfect corner to the edge of the area . . . where Scholes hit the ball first time on the volley.

— A BUSY YEAR —

Other things that happened in 1878, the year that United were formed:

- The Tokyo Stock Exchange was established.
- The Ottoman Empire ceded Cyprus to the United Kingdom.
- More than 640 died when the crowded pleasure boat *Princess Alice* collided with the *Bywell Castle* on the River Thames.
- The world's first recorded floodlit football fixture was played at Bramall Lane, Sheffield.
- Everton Football Club, then known as St Domingo, were formed.
- Joseph Stalin, later to be Soviet leader, was born.

— THE PEN IS MIGHTIER THAN THE BOOT —

Ten notable United player autobiographies:

Roy Keane, *The Autobiography* (2002)
The peerless United autobiography, Keane's book sold more copies in Ireland than any other book except *The Bible*. Gripping from the start, the prose, crafted by Ireland's best known journalist, Eamon Dunphy, is charged and brutally honest.

Sir Alex Ferguson, *Managing My Life* (1999)
Released a couple of months after the treble, the timing couldn't have been better. Nor could Ferguson's choice of Hugh McIlvanney as his ghost writer. A number one bestseller for months, Fergie's tome is forthright and revealing. Not that Brian Kidd should, or would, agree.

Jaap Stam, *Head to Head* (2001)
Was it the first autobiography which led to a player being directly sold? Dutch frankness might work in Maastricht, but not in Manchester where Sir Alex Ferguson's hawk eyes survey all. Despite the headlines, an insipid read.

Dwight Yorke, *Dwight Yorke: The Official Biography* (1999)
An authorised biography by Hunter Davies sounded like a good idea . . . by people who'd never met Dwight. Esteemed author Davies, buoyed by a healthy advance, put the hours in and travelled to Tobago to meet Yorke's family and friends. They were all happy to talk openly, unlike a disinterested Dwight. Davies' prose is engaging, but it doesn't compensate for Yorke's guard being higher than the list of notches on his bed posts.

Nobby Stiles, *After The Ball* (2003)
A beautifully ghosted autobiography by James Lawton, the story of a working-class hero told vividly. From Collyhurst trouble and strife, to *This Is Your Life*.

Harry Gregg, *Harry's Game* (2002)
Don't be put off by his old school mindset (Gregg admits he is a modern day Victor Meldrew). Gregg's description of the Munich air crash, in which the former United 'keeper rescued other passengers, is more visceral than any other.

Denis Law, various
The King of the Stretford End has almost got as many books to his name as goals. Law's 1969 *Book of Soccer* must have sold well, his 1979 autobiography too, because decades after he finished playing, Law bought out another autobiography in 1999. And then another in 2003 . . .

Norman Whiteside, *My Memories of Man United* (2003)
The story of growing up on Belfast's Shankill Road and playing for club and country while your mates are still at school should have been a great one. Yet Whiteside didn't want to say a bad word about anyone. Which begs the question: why do a book?

Eric Cantona, *My Story* (1993)
Originally published in France under the title *Un Rêve Modeste et Fou*, Cantona's life story was translated into English by Gorge Scanlon, his interpreter at Old Trafford. Given the rich subject matter, Eric is unusually reticent – perhaps because he'd been at Old Trafford for less than a year.

Mark Hughes, *Sparky – Barcelona, Bayern & Back* (1989)
Possibly the worst United player autobiography to hit the printing presses. A hardback containing just 96 pages, Hughes was as insightful in print as Peter Schmeichel in a television studio. Luckily, he's improved.

— LOYAL SERVANTS REWARDED —

Five testimonials played at Old Trafford:

Player	Opposition	Date
John Aston	All Star X1	April 25th 1956
Tony Dunne	Manchester City	October 24th 1973
Cliff Lloyd	England v Scotland	May 4th 1981
Mike Duxbury	Manchester City	August 13th 1989
Norman Whiteside	Everton	May 3rd 1992

— WORLDLY GOODS —

Following his death after the Munich disaster, Duncan Edwards left the sum of £4,368 (£4,050 9s 6d net).

— PACKING THEM IN —

Top ten away attendances for United games:

Year	Attendance	Competition	Result
1957	135,000	European Cup semi-final	Real Madrid 3 United 1
1968	125,000	European Cup semi-final	Real Madrid 3 United 3
1994	114,273	Champions League final	Barcelona 4 United 0
1968	105,000	European Cup quarter-final	Gornik Zabrze 1 United 0
1958	80,000	European Cup semi-final	Milan 4 United 0
1969	80,000	European Cup semi-final	Milan 2 United 0
1999	79,528	Champions League quarter-final	Inter 1 United 1
2005	78,957	Champions League second round	Milan 1 United 0
1954	77,920	FA Cup fifth round	Everton 2 United 1
2007	77,000	Champions League quarter-final	Roma 2 United 1

— FOGGED OFF —

United were due to play West Bromwich Albion at Old Trafford on December 22nd 1956. The crowd were present, as were the United players, referee and linesmen. But there was no West Bromwich team, nor any sign of the United manager Matt Busby.

The problem was that thick fog had enveloped the Midlands, delaying the visiting team, while Busby was stranded at Crewe as he returned from Brussels where he had been watching Anderlecht, United's forthcoming European Cup opponents. West Bromwich finally made Manchester at 4pm, by which time everyone had got fed up waiting and gone home.

— RED BRIEFS —

The briefest single Old Trafford appearance by a United player is six minutes, made by Paul Wratten against Wimbledon on April 2nd 1991.

— THE QUEEN'S SUMMER —

In the summer of 1953, an eight-club tournament was held in Glasgow to coincide with the coronation of Queen Elizabeth II. United played alongside Rangers, Celtic, Hibernian, Aberdeen, Tottenham Hotspur, Newcastle and Arsenal, with Hampden Park and Ibrox as venues. Due to their involvement, United's board decided to forgo a close season tour, as had become the norm in the immediate post-war era.

Manager Matt Busby took his players north a week before they were due to face Rangers in their first round tie, basing themselves at Troon on the Ayrshire coast, while provisional arrangements had been made to remain there until May 20th, the date of the final.

The first game against Scottish League and Cup winners Rangers was expected to attract more than 100,000 to Hampden's vast terraces, but there were 'only' 75,546 to see United win 2–1. The result restored some credibility to English football while also preventing a Scottish treble, following the defeats of Arsenal and Tottenham Hotspur by Celtic and Hibs.

United lost 2–1 to eventual winners Celtic in the semi-final in front of another huge crowd of 73,436. That game marked the end of Johnny Carey's United career as he announced his retirement just over a week later. The 34-year-old United captain had crossed the Irish Sea aged 17 in 1936, joining the club from St James's Gate, a Dublin junior club, for a fee of £250.

It was money well spent, as Carey went on to give United sterling service in a number of positions (including goalkeeper), leading them to league and FA Cup success in his 344 games. Carey also represented Ireland and the Republic of Ireland, as well as captaining a 'Rest of Europe' XI.

— GOOD DEED —

While in Hungary for United's UEFA Cup tie against Raba Gyor in 1984, chairman Martin Edwards and club director Maurice Watkins went for a walk when they came across a policeman struggling with a girl on a bridge, who was on the other side of the railings trying to break free and jump into the water.

The policeman shouted for help and the two United officials grabbed an arm each and pulled the girl back over the railings. Both men then walked away as the policeman tried to calm the girl down.

— RED POWER —

Tony Blair has overseen more United championships than any other British Prime Minister. And, thanks to Blair's long tenure at 10 Downing Street, United are most likely to win the league when the Labour party is in power.

Year	Prime Minister	Party
1908	Herbert Asquith	Liberal
1911	Herbert Asquith	Liberal
1952	Winston Churchill	Conservative
1956	Sir Anthony Eden	Conservative
1957	Harold Macmillan	Conservative
1965	Harold Wilson	Labour
1967	Harold Wilson	Labour
1993*	John Major	Conservative
1994*	John Major	Conservative
1996*	John Major	Conservative
1997*	Tony Blair	Labour
1999*	Tony Blair	Labour
2000*	Tony Blair	Labour
2001*	Tony Blair	Labour
2003*	Tony Blair	Labour
2007*	Tony Blair	Labour

*Premiership seasons

— GIGGSY DUVETS, ANYONE? —

The United megastore has been in six different locations. A small hut beside the railway was the original site, later moving to just along from where the away fans enter the ground now in the South Stand. It then moved across the forecourt again to the current site of the merchandising office. Next stop was down behind the Stretford End as United's merchandise boom took off in the early 1990s, before the store moved to temporary accommodation in the main car park opposite its present site.

— OLD TRAFFORD EVENTS —

Over the years, Old Trafford has been more than the home of Manchester United and a football stadium:

- During the First World War, American troops played baseball at the ground, while the Manchester County Police held their annual sports meetings there in 1925 and 1926.
- The following year, 1927, saw Ladies Wimbledon champion Suzanne Lenglen play a series of exhibition games, but attendances were poor.
- Rugby league is now a regular feature on the Old Trafford schedule, but the first such fixture was back in November 1958, when Salford played Leeds in a league fixture, with the local club having hired the ground as they wanted to try a match under floodlights. A crowd of around 8,000 saw the Yorkshire side win 22–17.
- In 1981, cricket's Lambert and Butler Cup was contested at the ground.
- In 1993 Old Trafford was the venue for the World Super-Middleweight Professional Boxing Championship between Chris Eubank and Nigel Benn. Over 40,000 packed the ground for a bout which was billed as 'Judgement Day' and millions more watched on TV. A thrilling contest ended in a draw.
- Songs of Praise echoed around Old Trafford in September 1994, but the singing was not for any United victory, but hymns sung by a large congregation for the BBC's television programme of the same name.
- Rock concerts starring the likes of Rod Stewart, Status Quo and Simply Red have also taken place at the ground.
- On the evening of February 10th 1958, the coffins of Roger Byrne, Eddie Colman, Geoff Bent, Mark Jones and Tommy Taylor, along with those of Bert Whalley, Walter Crickmere, Tom Curry, Alf Clarke and Tom Jackson who died in the Munich disaster were transported from Manchester's Ringway airport to Old Trafford, where they lay for the night in the gymnasium.

— CROWD HIGHS AND LOWS —

The five highest average home attendances pre-war:

1. 35,525 (1920/21)
2. 32,332 (1936/37)
3. 30,365 (1938/39)
4. 28, 510 (1921/22)
5. 27,995 (1924/25)

. . . and the five lowest:

1. 11,685 (1930/31)
2. 11,950 (1914/15)
3. 13,011 (1931/32)
4. 18,338 (1933/34)
5. 18,599 (1929/30)

— ALIEN INVASION! —

In 1990, the American newspaper *The National Enquirer* reported: "At a recent Manchester United home fixture, 47,000 fans were scared out of their wits and screamed in terror, when a UFO hovered above them. Within seconds, they were shrieking in panic and pointing to the sky. Players were running in a frantic daze, aware that they were being watched by aliens."

The incident didn't make the news in Britain – because it didn't happen . . . unless the reporter was taking a new angle on Wimbledon's long ball game.

— BEAM BACK FIRST —

The first Division One game to be shown live on closed-circuit television was Arsenal v United on Friday March 3rd 1967. A crowd of 28,423 watched the game beamed back from Highbury onto seven 40ft x 30ft screens erected at Old Trafford. The game was played on the Friday night as the League Cup final between Queens Park Rangers and West Bromwich Albion was to be played at Wembley the following day. The match at Highbury ended in a 1–1 draw.

— ODD PROGRAMME ISSUES —

- There was no *United Review* printed for the home fixture against Blackpool on February 22nd 1947 because of a printers' strike.
- During the 1948 FA Cup campaign, United were drawn at home against Liverpool, but the match was switched to Goodison Park, as Manchester City – whose ground United were sharing because of Old Trafford's bomb damage – were also drawn at home. The match programme was not a *United Review*, but a Liverpool issue.

— HEAD RED —

Warren Bradley, who played for United between 1958 and 1962 and was capped three times by England, was a reluctant footballer. As a child, his ambition was to be a headmaster.

Prior to playing for United, Bradley was successful with non-league Bishop Auckland, where he won 11 caps at England amateur level and two FA Amateur Cup winner's medals.

His fine form got him a move to Old Trafford – he thought as a reserve player. Bradley even took a job as a teacher in Manchester, while training part-time with United. Yet the Munich air crash rendered United short of players and he played 66 games, scoring 21 times. In 1968 he realised his ambition by becoming a headmaster at Lostock Comprehensive in Stretford. He died in 2007.

— FIRST EURO AWAY —

United's first European tour was in 1908, when they went to Hungary, Czechoslovakia and Austria, playing eight games.

— FORGOTTEN OPPONENTS —

Five early Newton Heath opponents that United never played:

Pendleton Olympic
Manchester Arcadians
Bootle Wanderers
Oughtrington Park
Earlston

— ON TO BETTER THINGS —

Five Reds players who won their first international caps after leaving United:

Stan Ackerley, Australia
Jimmy Rimmer, England
Eamon Dunphy, Republic of Ireland
Ted MacDougall, Scotland
Robbie Savage, Wales

— SELLING UP —

Bill Foulkes sold his European Cup winners medal in October 1992 at Christies in Glasgow. It was sold for £12,100. His jersey from the match went for £1,980.

— RAM OR RED? —

Prior to signing for United in 1972, Ian Storey-Moore was paraded at Derby's Baseball Ground as their 'new signing' from Nottingham Forest. A few days later, the winger joined United.

— CUP FINAL SING SONG —

Ten songs from the Community Singing song sheet for the 1948 FA Cup final between Manchester United and Blackpool:

'If You Were The Only Girl In The World'
'She's A Lassie From Lancashire'
'Loch Lomond'
'Land Of Hope and Glory'
'She'll Be Comin' Round the Mountain'
'Pack Up Your Troubles'
'John Brown's Body'
'I Do Like To Be Beside the Seaside'
'You Are My Sunshine'
'It's A Long Way to Tipperary'

— WHAT'S ON THE MENU? —

A selection of United dinner function menus:

1951/52 Championship dinner and dance
Crème Ambassadeur
Poulet De Grain Mascotte
Peches Mon Desir

1968 European Cup final after match celebrations at the Hotel Russell, London
Crème d'Asperges
Supreme de Volaille Jeanette
Jambon d'York
Dindonneau de Norfolk
Gateau Glace Vanille

1975 Second Division Championship dinner dance at the Midland Hotel, Manchester
Supreme de Saumon Neptune
Contrefilet de Boeuf Poele
Peche Glacee Cardinal

1977 FA Cup final banquet at Royal Lancaster Hotel, London
Cream of Chicken Soup
Fillet of Sole
Roast Sirloin of Beef
Vanilla Bombe

1999 FA Cup gala dinner at Royal Lancaster Hotel, London
Fillet of Sea Bass with a Fennel, Tomato and Basil Sauce
Roasted Fillet of Scottish Beef
Strawberry Mousse

1999 UEFA Champions League after match buffet
Selection of sliced meats to include Jamon Serrano and tomato bread
Prawns cocktail with lemon and spicy sauce
Merluza filet with romesco sauce
English truffle
Crema Catalana

2000/2001 Premier League Championship Banquet in the Manchester Suite, Old Trafford
Royal Greenland Prawns on a Julienne of Iceberg Lettuce
Seared Fillet of Beef with a Shallot and Port Sauce
Pannacotta with Fruit Coulis

— WHERE'S THE TESTIMONIAL? —

Only John Aston, Brian Kidd and Nobby Stiles of the 1968 European Cup-winning side did not receive a benefit match at some point in their careers. Shay Brennan, David Sadler and George Best all had theirs after leaving the club.

— IT'S OLD TRAFFORD, BUT NO UNITED —

Five post-war non-United FA Cup replays at Old Trafford:

1955, Bury 2 Stoke City 3, third round fourth replay
1958, Rochdale 1 Hartlepool United 2, first round second replay
1962, Liverpool 0 Preston North End 1, fifth round second replay
1964, Barrow 0 Grimsby Town 2, first round second replay
1970, Barnsley 0 Rhyl 2, second round second replay

Five pre-war semi finals played at Old Trafford:

1910, Barnsley 3 Everton 0, replay
1914, Sheffield United 0 Burnley 0
1921, Wolverhampton Wanderers 3 Cardiff City 1, replay
1923, Bolton Wanderers 1 Sheffield Wednesday 0
1928, Huddersfield Town 2 Sheffield United 2

Five international fixtures played at Old Trafford:

April 17th 1926, England 0 Scotland 1
November 16th 1938, England 7 Ireland 0
July 13th 1966, Hungary 1 Portugal 3 (World Cup)
May 28th 1991, Argentina 1 Russia 1 (English Challenge Cup)
June 19th 1996, Italy 0 Germany 0 (Euro '96)

— GHOST GROUNDS —

Six grounds from the old Football League First Division that United do not visit today:

Roker Park, Sunderland
Maine Road, Manchester
Ayresome Park, Middlesbrough
Highbury Stadium, London
The Dell, Southampton
Plough Lane, Wimbledon

Oh, and of course Elland Road, Leeds.

— JOHNNY OF ALL TRADES —

A team of United players who could play in more than one position:

1. Johnny Carey (goalkeeper, full-back, half-back, forward)
2. Roger Byrne (full-back, outside-left)
3. Johnny Aston (full-back, inside and centre forward)
4. Jackie Blanchflower (goalkeeper, wing-half, centre half, inside forward)
5. Mike Duxbury (full-back, wing-half, inside forward)
6. Clayton Blackmore (full-back, half-back, forward)
7. John O'Shea (full-back, centre-back, midfield, striker, goalkeeper)
8. Bryan Robson (midfield, central defender)
9. David Sadler (centre-half, wing-half, centre forward, inside forward)
10. John Fitpatrick (full-back, wing-half, inside forward)
11. Duncan Edwards (anywhere)

— NORN IRON REDS —

Five United players featured in the Northern Ireland starting line-up for six games in the late 1970s: Sammy McIlroy, Jimmy Nicholl, David McCreery, Tommy Jackson and Chris Mcgrath. Former Reds George Best (then of Fulham) and Trevor Anderson (then at Swindon) also featured. Liverpool, meanwhile, haven't had one player from Northern Ireland since goalkeeper Elisha Scott in the 1930s.

— GOALS GALORE —

Five high scoring home European ties:

United 7 Roma 1	2006/07	Champions League
United 6 Djurgardens1	1964/65	Inter Cities Fairs Cup
United 10 Anderlecht 0	1956/57	European Cup
United 6 Helsinki 0	1965/66	European Cup
United 7 Waterford 1	1968/69	European Cup

Five high scoring home FA Cup ties:

United 7 Accrington Stanley 0	1902/03
United 6 Blackburn Rovers 1	1908/09
United 8 Yeovil 0	1948/49
United 7 Staple Hill 2	1905/06
United 6 West Ham United 0	2002/03

— THE JOY OF SIX —

In September 1959, United scored six goals on two occasions – 6–3 v Chelsea away on Setember 2nd and 6–0 v Leeds United at home seven days later. The following season, the Reds once again took six goals off Chelsea, this time at home, on December 26th 1960 and five days later hit Manchester City for five at home.

Strangely, less than a month later, United conceded six against Leicester City on January 21st 1961 and seven against Sheffield Wednesday in the FA Cup on February 1st 1961.

— FIRING BLANKS —

In the relegation season of 1973/74, United failed to score in any of their final three games. They also had a run of three goalless games between March 13th and March 23rd.

Season 1980/81, meanwhile, saw a run of five goalless games between February 7th and March 7th made up of 1–0 defeats to Leicester, Manchester City, Leeds and Southampton and a 0–0 draw with Tottenham. Even the pre-war relegation seasons did not see such a poor return. Thankfully, the depressing run came to an end with a bang when United drew 3–3 away to Aston Villa on March 14th 1981.

— RARE PROGRAMMES —

A selection of the most sought after United programmes:

Preston North End (Lancs Cup), Home, No 8, October 30th 1946
A low key match which attracted a low attendance, and so the programme is in short supply.

Sheffield Wednesday (FA Cup), Home, No 21, February 19th 1958
The first game after the Munich disaster and a match programme collected by many non-United supporters. The programme is also notable for the United match line-up containing eleven blank spaces. Copies with the spaces remaining blank are worth considerably more than those with the names of those who did play filled in. Although widely sought after, it is not too expensive to obtain and usually sells for £120–£150.

Red Star Belgrade (European Cup), Away, February 5th 1958
The last game before the Munich air crash, making it the 'penny black' of United programmes. It is not the most expensive to obtain and would cost you between £1500 and £2000.

Anderlecht (European Cup), Away, September 12th 1956
This was United's first European fixture and the programme is certainly more difficult to come by than the Red Star one (above). A copy would certainly cost you more.

Wolverhampton Wanderers (Division One, postponed), Home, No 20, February 8th 1958
This match was due to be played three days after the match in Belgrade and was obviously postponed. Due to printing deadlines, the programme was in production on the day of the Munich crash, but when the news began to filter through and the game was called off, all copies were meant to have been destroyed. Some, however, were kept by workers at the printers. How many is unknown. This programme would fetch at least four figures at auction.

Portsmouth (Division One, postponed), Home, No 13, December 21st 1946
Another postponed issue, with the game called off at the last moment after the programme had been printed. Again, some survived, and again you would have to pay well into four figures.

Benfica (European Cup Final replay), Highbury, Friday May 31st 1968
A programme for a match that never took place. However, had United drawn with Benfica in the 1968 European Cup Final, then a replay was due to be held at Highbury on Friday May 31st (just two days later). A programme was put together (similar to the normal Arsenal issue of the time) in case the match took place and some were printed off and kept by workers and also contractors who were working at the printers at the time.

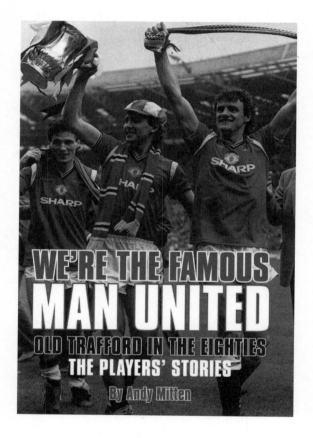

WE'RE THE FAMOUS
MAN UNITED
OLD TRAFFORD IN THE EIGHTIES
THE PLAYERS' STORIES
By Andy Mitten

www.visionsp.co.uk

— UNITED'S SEASON BY SEASON RECORD —

Note: Newton Heath were not admitted into the league until season 1892-93.

Season	(Div)	P	W	D	L	F	A	Pts	Pos.
1892/93	1	30	6	6	18	50	85	18	16th (bottom)
1893/94	1	30	6	2	22	36	72	14	16th (bottom)
1894/95	2	30	15	8	7	78	44	38	3rd
1895/96	2	30	15	3	12	66	57	33	6th
1896/97	2	30	17	5	8	56	34	39	2nd
1897/98	2	30	16	6	8	64	35	38	4th
1898/99	2	34	19	5	10	67	43	43	4th
1899/00	2	34	20	4	10	63	27	44	4th
1900/01	2	34	14	4	16	42	38	32	10th
1901/02	2	34	11	6	17	38	53	28	15th
1902/03	2	34	15	8	11	53	38	38	5th
1903/04	2	34	20	8	6	65	33	48	3rd
1904/05	2	34	24	5	5	81	30	53	3rd
1905/06	2	38	28	6	4	90	28	62	2nd (promoted)
1906/07	1	38	17	8	13	53	56	42	8th
1907/08	1	38	23	6	9	81	48	52	1st
1908/09	1	38	15	7	16	58	68	37	13th
1909/10	1	38	19	7	12	69	61	45	5th
1910/11	1	38	22	8	8	72	40	52	1st
1911/12	1	38	13	11	14	45	60	37	13th
1912/13	1	38	19	8	11	69	43	46	4th
1913/14	1	38	15	6	17	52	62	36	14th
1914/15	1	38	9	12	17	46	62	30	18th
FIRST WORLD WAR									
1919/20	1	42	13	14	15	54	50	40	12th
1922/23	1	42	17	14	11	51	36	48	4th
1923/24	1	42	13	14	15	52	44	40	12th
1924-25	1	42	23	11	8	57	23	57	2nd
1925/26	1	42	19	6	17	66	73	44	9th
1926/27	1	42	13	14	15	52	64	40	15th
1927/28	1	42	16	7	19	72	80	39	18th
1928/29	1	42	14	13	15	66	76	41	12th
1929/30	1	42	15	8	19	67	88	38	17th
1930/31	1	42	7	8	27	53	115	22	22nd (relegated)
1931/32	2	42	17	8	17	71	72	42	12th
1932/33	2	42	15	13	14	71	68	43	6th

Season	(Div)	P	W	D	L	F	A	Pts	Pos.
1934/35	2	42	23	4	15	76	55	50	5th
1935/36	2	42	22	12	8	85	43	56	1st (promoted)
1936/37	1	42	10	12	20	55	78	32	21st (relegated)
1937/38	2	42	22	9	11	82	50	53	2nd (promoted)
1938/39	1	42	11	16	15	57	65	38	14th
			SECOND	WORLD	WAR				
1946/47	1	42	22	12	8	95	54	56	2nd
1947/48	1	42	19	14	9	81	48	52	2nd
1948/49	1	42	21	11	10	77	44	53	2nd
1949/50	1	42	18	14	10	69	44	50	4th
1950/51	1	42	24	8	10	74	40	56	2nd
1951/52	1	42	23	11	8	95	52	57	1st
1952/53	1	42	18	10	14	69	72	46	8th
1953/54	1	42	18	12	12	73	58	48	4th
1954/55	1	42	20	7	15	84	74	47	5th
1955/56	1	42	25	10	7	83	51	60	1st
1956/57	1	42	28	8	6	103	54	64	1st
1957/58	1	42	16	11	15	85	75	43	9th
1958/59	1	42	24	7	9	103	66	55	2nd
1959/60	1	42	19	7	16	102	80	45	7th
1960/61	1	42	18	9	15	88	76	45	7th
1961/62	1	42	15	9	18	72	75	39	15th
1962/63	1	42	12	10	20	67	81	34	19th
1963/64	1	42	23	7	12	90	62	53	2nd
1964/65	1	42	26	9	7	89	39	61	1st
1965/66	1	42	18	15	9	84	59	51	4th
1966/67	1	42	24	12	6	84	45	60	1st
1967/68	1	42	24	8	10	89	55	56	2nd
1968/69	1	42	15	12	15	57	53	42	11th
1969/70	1	42	14	17	11	66	61	45	8th
1970/71	1	42	16	11	15	65	66	43	8th
1971/72	1	42	19	10	13	69	61	48	8th
1972/73	1	42	12	13	17	44	60	37	18th
1973/74	1	42	10	12	20	38	48	32	21st (relegated)
1974/75	2	42	26	9	7	66	30	61	1st (promoted)
1975/76	1	42	23	10	9	68	42	56	3rd
1976/77	1	42	18	11	13	71	62	47	6th
1977/78	1	42	16	10	16	67	63	42	10th
1978/79	1	42	15	15	12	60	63	45	9th
1979/80	1	42	24	10	8	65	35	58	2nd
1980/81	1	42	15	18	9	51	36	48	8th

Season	(Div)	P	W	D	L	F	A	Pts	Pos.
1981/82	1	42	22	12	8	59	29	78	3rd
1982/83	1	42	19	13	10	56	38	70	3rd
1983/84	1	42	20	14	8	71	41	74	4th
1984/85	1	42	22	10	10	77	47	76	4th
1985/86	1	42	22	10	10	70	36	76	4th
1986/87	1	42	14	14	14	52	45	56	11th
1987/88	1	40	23	12	5	71	38	81	2nd
1988/89	1	38	13	12	13	45	35	51	11th
1989/90	1	38	13	9	16	46	47	48	13th
1990/91	1	38	16	12	10	58	45	59	6th
1991/92	1	42	21	15	6	63	33	78	2nd
1992/93	1	42	24	12	6	67	31	84	1st
1993/94	1	42	27	11	4	80	38	92	1st
1994/95	1	42	26	10	6	77	28	88	2nd
1995/96	1	38	25	7	6	73	35	82	1st
1996/97	1	38	21	12	5	76	44	75	1st
1997/98	1	38	23	8	7	73	26	77	2nd
1998/99	1	38	22	13	3	80	37	79	1st
1999/00	1	38	28	7	3	97	45	91	1st
2000/01	1	38	24	8	6	79	31	80	1st
2001/02	1	38	24	5	9	87	45	77	3rd
2002/03	1	38	25	8	5	74	34	83	1st
2003/04	1	38	23	6	9	64	35	75	3rd
2004/05	1	38	22	11	5	58	26	77	2nd
2005/06	1	38	25	8	5	72	34	83	2nd
2006/07	1	38	28	5	5	83	27	89	1st